# The Wonder Worker

Jesus in the Book of Mark

Jim Inkster

Published by 5 Smooth Stones

The right of Jim Inkster to be identified as the authors of the Work has been asserted by them in accordance with the Copyright, Designs and Patents Act 1988 All rights reserved. No part of this publication may be reproduced, stored in a retrieval system, or transmitted, in any form or by any means without the prior permission of the publisher, nor be otherwise circulated in any form of binding or cover other than that in which it is published and without a similar condition being imposed on the subsequent purchaser.

Kelowna, BC

Canada

All rights reserved.

ISBN:0956334288
ISBN-13:9780956334282

## DEDICATION

To all those who are seeking first The Wonder Worker

# CONTENTS

|    | The Wonder Worker     | 1      |
|----|-----------------------|--------|
| 1  | Mark Chapter One      | Pg 5   |
| 2  | Mark Chapter Two      | Pg 14  |
| 3  | Mark Chapter Three    | Pg 19  |
| 4  | Mark Chapter Four     | Pg 27  |
| 5  | Mark Chapter Five     | Pg 41  |
| 6  | Mark Chapter Six      | Pg 49  |
| 7  | Mark Chapter Seven    | Pg 66  |
| 8  | Mark Chapter Eight    | Pg 73  |
| 9  | Mark Chapter Nine     | Pg 85  |
| 10 | Mark Chapter Ten      | Pg 96  |
| 11 | Mark Chapter Eleven   | Pg 105 |
| 12 | Mark Chapter Twelve   | Pg 117 |
| 13 | Mark Chapter Thirteen | Pg 126 |
| 14 | Mark Chapter Fourteen | Pg 137 |
| 15 | Mark Chapter Fifteen  | Pg 150 |
| 16 | Mark Chapter Sixteen  | Pg 155 |

# ACKNOWLEDGMENTS

Scriptures taken from the Holy Bible, New International Version®, NIV®. Copyright © 1973, 1978, 1984, 2011 by Biblica, Inc.™ Used by permission of Zondervan. All rights reserved worldwide. www.zondervan.com The "NIV" and "New International Version" are trademarks registered in the United States Patent and Trademark Office by Biblica, Inc.™

The Wonder Worker

# THE WONDER WORKER

Jesus is the Wonder Worker, even today, for Jesus said in Matthew 28:20: "And surely I am with you always, to the very end of the age." He is with us. Mark 16 ends with: "Then the disciples went out and preached everywhere, and the Lord worked with them and confirmed his word by the signs that accompanied it." In fact Jesus constantly astounded the people with signs and wonders. They would say He is not like our teachers for He teaches with authority. John 7: 31 states: 'Still, many in the crowd put their faith in him. They said, "When the Christ comes, will he do more miraculous signs than this man?"

Jesus, speaking of Himself, said in John 14:11: "Believe me when I say that I am in the Father and the Father is in me; or at least believe on the evidence of the miracles themselves." Jesus did not come with words only. He preached repent for the Kingdom of God is at hand and then demonstrated it. His works were the validation of His words.

The book of Mark focuses on Jesus as a man of action. The phrase "at once" or the word "immediately" is used more than thirty times in this book to describe events. It is a book with the stress on action and facts rather than themes or topics. Both Matthew and Luke use far more verses to describe the same events as Mark. For example Luke uses 23 verses to describe John the Baptist's ministry to Mark's 10. If you are an action person, one who wants to do rather than talk, this is the book for you. Jesus puts wings to His words!

In reading Mark over numerous times and in different translations the main impressions that jumped out is the Kingdom of God and faith. This book so clearly shows one kingdom invading and overthrowing another. Jesus came to destroy the works of the devil and it was evident to the common people. His actions were the confirmation of his preaching. He not only preached the Kingdom of God, He showed the Kingdom of God. As Jesus disrupted Satan's kingdom Satan's minions reacted.

The other revelation that comes forth is the issue of faith. This book shows that the Kingdom of God is produced through faith. The religious system talked the talk but didn't bring any evidence of God's Kingdom. They bound people with legalism and alienated them from God through judgment. Jesus came with authority, which operated through faith. Faith is a fact but faith is also an act. James says in chapter 2 and verse 18: "I will show you my faith by what I do." Faith in God produces results. Results amaze people!

The Wonder Worker will astound you too as you read through this commentary and the gospel of Mark. Even more amazing is the fact that He wants us to do the same things He did. We are to preach the Kingdom of God is at hand and demonstrate it with signs, wonders and miracles following. Pray as you read this book that God would breathe upon the words releasing revelation to you. When we know that we know something, who can stop us from living it out. Let the Wonder Worker described in Mark captivate your heart and empower you for great works as He promised.

Please have your bible with you as you read so that you can read the portion of scripture referred to within the chapter.

# MARK CHAPTER ONE

# PART ONE

**I baptize you with water…" vs. 8**

Mark starts his gospel with the ministry of John the Baptist. John was essential to the ministry of Christ. He fulfilled Isaiah's prophecy of a voice calling in the desert: "prepare the way of the Lord, make straight paths for him". There was an anointing and call upon his life from birth to complete this role. He didn't do it out of his own strength, talent, gifts, good looks or personal motivation. He could do it because the Spirit of the Lord enabled him to. The favor and the presence of the Lord gifts you with the ability to impact people's lives. Without His favor you can preach and prophesy and sing and dance with the best of them and no one will pay any attention to you.


John was making straight paths before Jesus through his preaching. He preached repentance for the forgiveness of sins and people responded by being baptized in water. Repentance means to change your mind. Changing your mind about how you perceive the world will change how you respond to your world. Interestingly his message wasn't repentance from sin but repentance in regard to forgiveness of sin. People understand sin whether they want to acknowledge it or not. The problem isn't the existence of sin but the consequences of sin. When we recognize our sin, we feel judgment that leaves us in despair, as we are incapable of satisfying that judgment. We have no means of atonement within ourselves. This is overwhelming so we try to ignore it, rationalize it away, and create scientific or philosophical theories that we hope will eradicate the guilt. Hiding was the first thing Adam did after he sinned. What else can we do?


John didn't preach turn from sin. He preached repentance for the forgiveness of sins. People needed to change their minds about forgiveness. They lived under a religious system that created an untenable, unbearable web of judgment not freedom. The more they tried to fulfill the law the less successful they were.  They saw no escape from judgment, only failure to please God.  Judgment is a harsh taskmaster.  These people needed to know there was hope.  They needed to know there was forgiveness.  They knew they couldn't master sin, in fact, that it had mastered them.  What John did was give them hope.  He straightened out their thinking on whom God was and what he was going to do for them.  God doesn't want to condemn and destroy men, He wants to restore and love mankind.  Sin makes people morally crooked and twisted.  Sin is birthed in our minds before it is acted out.  People needed to have their minds enlightened regarding God's ability to forgive.

# PART TWO

**"but He will baptize you with the Holy Spirit." Verse 8**

John's role was to make straight paths before the Lord.  His preaching led to people repenting, receiving forgiveness for sins and being water baptized.  Water symbolizes cleansing but as Paul said in Romans 6 it also represents death.  Have you ever pondered what death is? I used to think it meant ceasing to exist or even annihilation. It, in fact, means separation. Physical death is separation of the spirit from the body. Spiritual death is separation of your spirit from God's spirit. The people who responded to John's message were not only cleansed from sin but in effect were also saying I am dead to that old way of life.

Jesus came with a baptism of the Holy Spirit. Romans 8:11 says: "And if the Spirit of him who raised Jesus from the dead is living in you, he who raised Christ from the dead will also give life to your mortal bodies through his Spirit, who lives in you." For man this is impossible but for God all things are possible. Jesus not only died in our place, he rose from the dead. This is crucial to our understanding as Christians. Jesus is not dead; He is alive. He is not separated from God but united with Him. We have this hope. Death has no victory over us. Our mortal body may pass away but our spirit man lives and will receive a new immortal body.

Jesus came not just to call us to repentance regarding forgiveness of sins but also to release the Holy Spirit and His power into our lives. We are not powerless. We have the same power that raised a man who was dead 3 days from the grave. This power operated in Jesus' life from the time of his baptism with John to His resurrection. It was the Holy Spirit that released authority through Jesus. Mark 1 verse 22 says: "The people were amazed at his teaching, because he taught them as one who had authority, not as the teachers of the Law." This authority spilled over into healing and driving out of demons. Throughout the book of Mark Jesus is driving out demons.

For Christians to ignore the baptism of the Holy Spirit is equivalent to going to war without ammunition or into the boxing ring with our hands tied behind our back. We are relatively ineffective. We need to embrace the baptism; the empowering of the Holy Spirit, if we are going to live and live abundantly the life Jesus promised us.

Mark was an action man. He wanted to know what the bottom line is. With this in mind he launched his narrative with the role of John the Baptist and repentance, followed hotly by Jesus baptism with the Holy Spirit and the subsequent promise that we too will receive the same. He is saying we have to change our thinking about God's attitude to us. God loves us and forgives us. Our thinking needs to continue to be renewed to the fact that He also empowers us to live above and beyond what we have experienced to date. The word tells us we are in the world but not of the world. To live beyond what the world offers we have to grasp the reality of our complete forgiveness and the power of God that will not only be in us but envelope us entirely. The word "baptism" is a transliteration of the Greek word "baptizo" which means to submerge completely as cloth being immersed in dye. The Spirit permeates us and surrounds us.

To settle for anything less than to be completely immersed, surrounded and permeated with the Holy Spirit is to fall far short of the fullness of life available to us. This baptism empowers us to be liberators of those bound through the deception of the evil one. We can do what Jesus did and more if we believe!

# PART THREE

The introduction to Mark referred to two themes that had been highlighted: the Kingdom of God and faith. There is a definite clash of kingdoms throughout the ministry of Jesus. I John 3:8 says: "Jesus came to destroy the works of the evil one." We need to remember that. If the evil one can lull us into ignoring that he is real, he can continue to extend his kingdom. That kingdom is one of servitude and bondage. Jesus came to set us free. When Jesus began his ministry he preached the Kingdom of God is at hand. Through his birth and his life the kingdom of God or Heaven was invading earth.

One of the most amazing things about human beings is their adaptability to their environment: the Bedouins of the desert, the Inuit of the Arctic. Not only does mankind adapt to their physical environment they also adapt to their spiritual environment. They learn to live within its realms and to seek their own benefit by adapting to its demands. Often man gets so comfortable with his surroundings that he will fight to maintain the status quo than receive something far better. Jesus came preaching life, freedom, sight, acceptance and love – yet people rejected him in favour of their present condition.

Mark 1: 23 – 27 recounts one of the first encounters Jesus had with the other kingdom during public ministry. **"Just then a man in their synagogue who was possessed by an evil spirit cried out, "What do you want with us, Jesus of Nazareth? Have you come to destroy us? I know who you are--the Holy One of God!" "Be quiet!" said**

**Jesus sternly. "Come out of him!" The evil spirit shook the man violently and came out of him with a shriek. The people were all so amazed that they asked each other, "What is this? A new teaching--and with authority! He even gives orders to evil spirits and they obey him."** The verse before said the people were amazed with his teaching. This deliverance further convinced them of his authority.

Take note of the fact that this first demonic manifestation happened in the synagogue. The kingdom of darkness is often entrenched in religious systems of worship. The enemy is a counterfeiter not a creator. As he hates the Father he has set about to ensure that men do too. What better way than to pervert systems of worship! If these systems that proclaim they know God and speak for Him present an image of an angry God, then people will either fear Him or rebel against Him.

Jesus came using terms of endearment and speaking of love. He had to rebuke the religious leaders of the day over and over again as they so misrepresented His Father. He came to a people group, who had a great destiny but had lost their way, to set them free. The religious system did not want to lose the status quo.

They enjoyed their privileged positions of power. They went through rituals that all pointed to the one true God but failed to see Him when He came in the flesh. And the demonic powers that inspired and empowered that system manifest again and again when the Kingdom of God was demonstrated in power.

Those spirits still manifest through religious people today. They will try to kill and subject any move of God rather than allow revelation of the love of God to come forth.

Be alert and discerning. When the Kingdom of God comes, there is a clash.

# MARK CHAPTER TWO

# PART ONE

**Mark 2: 1 – 12** (Please read it for the full details)

The incident with the paralytic brings together the two themes of the book – faith and the Kingdom of God. (Jesus is teaching the people. I think it is important that the church generally gets their head around this. The teaching of the word is what Jesus did, the apostles, and Paul. The word taught with authority releases the presence and power of the Holy Spirit. If we want to see the kingdom of God coming in power, we need to preach and teach the word.) Four men are so determined to get their friend to Jesus they tear up another man's roof, most likely Peter's. Jesus doesn't rebuke them for the inappropriateness of their actions. He sees something more. He sees faith. In response to that faith He tells the man his sins are forgiven. This is where kingdom against kingdom clashes once again. This time it is a condition of the heart that is exposed, not a demon.

There were teachers of the law there. In their hearts they judged Jesus as a blasphemer. Only God can forgive sins! Oops! Did you happen to miss God sitting in your midst? The scripture says they were thinking to themselves. Only the Holy Spirit can search the heart of a man and He revealed it to Jesus. Could this not happen to us who are filled with the same Holy Spirit too?

To show them that the Son of Man has authority to forgive sins He told the paralytic to get up and go home. Sin and sickness walk hand in hand. Remember John preached a repentance of forgiveness of sins. He was preparing the way for people to receive the goodness of God expressed in forgiveness. The enemy's kingdom does not function on faith or extend compassion. It concentrates on legalities and knows no joy at extending mercy. The book of James says 'mercy triumphs over judgment' within the Kingdom of God. But the kingdom of darkness knows only judgment.

Notice that the four men's faith caused Jesus to respond with healing. It wasn't the paralytic's faith, nor was it Jesus' faith. The key is that someone had faith. Faith pleases God and He responses. Their faith also produced action. They didn't wait outside but pushed through into the presence of Jesus. Our faith needs action; action that will draws us into the center of God's presence. When we act on faith, we not only find ourselves before the Lord but we also are a source of pleasure to Him.

## PART TWO

In the last half of chapter 2 there are three confrontations Jesus has with the Pharisees: one, his openness to sinners and tax collectors, two, his disciples not fasting and three, picking grain to eat on the Sabbath. Each one of these incidents provoked indignation from the Pharisees and teachers of the law.

Jesus' response was: "No one sews a patch of

unshrunk cloth on an old garment. If he does, the new piece will pull away from the old, making the tear worse. And no one pours new wine into old wineskins. If he does, the wine will burst the skins, and both the wine and the wineskins will be ruined. No, he pours new wine into new wineskins." (Mark 2:21,22) This scripture is often used to explain why a fresh outpouring of the Holy Spirit creates new churches. But it says much more than that.

When people as a church or society are in transition to a new way of life, there is a tendency to try to repair the old one by adding something of the new. There is a reluctance to accept change. People like the status quo, the way it is. Why change? It worked well this way for so many years why do it differently? We try to preserve something of what was important to us rather than embracing something completely new. We want to patch up the old and keep it.

Personally, I am terrible at throwing out appliances that break down yet look as good as new. There is no point in trying to repair it, as the cost is far higher than replacing. But because I am fond of it and the pleasure it brought me, I can't get rid of it. The Law had a place. Paul says its role was to point us to Christ. The problem the Pharisees were having was accepting the new in place of the old. The new fulfilled all the requirements of the old so the old had become redundant. Jesus was the answer to the law. The Pharisees had spent their whole lives studying the law and embracing it that it became to them their source of life. Only Jesus could be that. But they just wanted to add Him onto what they had so they could keep what they had. Jesus said the new way would only make things worse for the old way of life. It couldn't be contained in the old religious system.

This is a continuing problem for the church. Paul said to the Galatians why having started in freedom through faith in Christ are you going back to trying to fulfill the law. Christ is not an addendum. He is the way, the truth and the life. He cannot be added to a legalistic system to make it better. His life flowing through it will create constant conflict, as the law was made for man, not man for the law.

# MARK CHAPTER THREE

# PART ONE

Mark 3 starts with the report of Jesus healing a man with a shriveled hand. Unfortunately for Him it happened on a Sabbath and in the synagogue. Why? Because this guaranteed the Pharisees would be there to see it and it would bring the warfare to the fore once again.

Verse 5 says he commanded the man to stretch forth his hand and when he did it was completely restored. A MIRACLE! No other description for it! Verse 6 says: "Then the Pharisees went out and began to plot with the Herodians how they might kill Jesus." Does this not seem a rather extreme reaction to a wonderful, caring, freeing miracle? Why would they want to kill a man for doing such good?

The Pharisees conspired with the Herodians to kill Jesus. This is the religious system working with the political system to suppress the plan of God. The political system is often stirred up by and the pawn of the religious system. Never underestimate the power of religion to move mankind to do its will. The very people who should have recognized the plans of God where bent on destroying them. They would have taught the people about the Messiah, His coming and His deliverance of Israel. Their teaching would have helped to some degree prepare the way for the coming Messiah. But they couldn't see Him before their very eyes.

Jesus was angry with them because they lacked compassion. They would rather have a person stay bound in sickness than violate their rules for the Sabbath. Verse 5 says He was deeply distressed at their stubborn hearts. This word, translated as stubborn in the NIV, is ***porosis***, which means the mind of one has been blunted, a) of stubbornness, obduracy. Stubbornness means showing dogged determination not to change one's attitude or position on something, especially in spite of good arguments or reasons to do so. The Pharisees' minds had been blunted by their religion. They were determined not to change even in the face of overwhelming evidence too. Obduracy usually connotes a stubborn resistance marked by harshness and lack of feeling. That seems to sum up the reaction of the Pharisees to something so wonderful as a completely restored hand. Their reaction was extremely harsh.

The word, porosis, also means covering with a callus. I used to play guitar when I was younger. The most painful part of learning guitar was the metal strings. They cut deeply into your fingertips, leaving you in agony over the next couple of days. If you persevered you were rewarded with a nice thick callus on the end of your finger. That callus protected your finger from further pain but it also blunted your ability to feel as sensitively through your fingertips. To hold onto their belief in the midst of the Roman Empire and its suppression probably developed a callus on their hearts. It protected them from pain and allowed them to hold fast to what they believed. But it also desensitized them to truly seeing God's plan.

A sensitive heart will be hurt. To deal with the pain we often harden our hearts toward people. The problem with this is it hardens our heart to Him as

He often speaks through people to us. We also lose our ability to respond with compassion. We can become harsh and unfeeling in the midst of a tremendous move of God. What a choice! Be sensitive and embrace the pain or be hard and miss the person of God!

# PART TWO

People were drawn to Jesus and followed him everywhere. He healed many, verse 10, and cast out demons, verse 11. The demons would cry out 'You are the Son of God' and He gave them strict orders not to tell who He was, verse 12. Why would He tell them to not say who He was? Deliverance is sometimes quite startling and attention grabbing. If the demons were declaring you are the Son of God as they flee, wouldn't that be a good thing? Surely it would shut the Pharisees and doubters up.

A similar incident is reported in Acts when Paul and Silas were in Philippi and the girl with a spirit of divination kept broadcasting that they were servants of the Most High God who are telling you the way to be saved. (Acts 16) Paul became very troubled by it so much so that he cast the spirit out of her. Again, why? She's helping to spread the gospel easier. She would have been known for her ability to predict the future. People would respect that and take her proclamations seriously. **But the source of revelation is as important as the revelation**. The wrong source skews the true revelation. It's tainted with the occult, the kingdom of darkness, not colored with the light of Heaven. Matthew 16:16 is a demonstration of heavenly revelation. Jesus said Peter didn't get this from man but from His Father in heaven. Upon this rock, revelation from the Father, is the church built and the gates of Hades cannot overcome it. Revelation is the basis of our faith. For it to be strong, it must come from the Father and no other source.

Mark constantly refers to the casting out of demons, especially connected to sickness. His gospel isn't very seeker sensitive but neither was Jesus. People need an encounter with a powerful God. Paul said in I Corinthians 2: 4, 5: "My message and my preaching were not with wise and persuasive words, but with a demonstration of the Spirit's power, so that your faith might not rest on men's wisdom, but on God's power." Our faith needs to rest on God's power. Then when men have forsaken you or failed you, your faith will endure for it is built upon the solid rock that cannot be shaken or shifted.

For people to know the gospel they need to witness the power of God's Spirit. Deliverance was a consistent sign to the people that the Kingdom of God was at hand. The enemy could not withstand the presence of God through His Holy Spirit. People may have many reactions to deliverance: fear, irritation, upset over a lack of dignity, whatever. But they will not be able to question a genuine power encounter with God. What do you want your faith built on: persuasive words of men or the power of God?

## PART THREE

From verse 13 to the end of the chapter Jesus appointed the 12 apostles, released them to preach and have authority over demons. He then encountered the attack of the Pharisees over the source of his authority while in the midst of so many people coming and going that they didn't have time to eat. Then, verse 21says: "When his family heard about this, they went to take charge of him, for they said, "He is out of his mind."

What did they hear about? Deliverance! The apostles were casting out demons under His authority, as was He. The Pharisees are accusing Him of doing deliverance in the power of Satan. Then His family turn up to take Him home as they think He's mad.

Deliverance causes all manner of response. People who are set free rejoice, people who are under the influence of the evil one complain and try to discredit it, and people who are unfamiliar with the demonic often think it's unreal. The bottom line is: it is real. It does set people free. The Pharisees saw their power base and influence over people waning, as they did not move in the authority that Jesus did. Deliverance is an exciting, 'in your face' experience. The enemy will do anything he can to preserve his kingdom. The full force of the enemy is released to stop those who are ministering in deliverance.

Jesus said in verse 29 and 30: "But whoever blasphemes against the Holy Spirit will never be forgiven; he is guilty of an eternal sin." He said this because they were saying, "He has an evil spirit." Accusing someone who does deliverance by the Holy Spirit of doing it by another power other than the Holy Spirit is to blaspheme the Holy Spirit. Blaspheme is a transliterated word that means to speak evil of. The Pharisees were speaking evil of the Holy Spirit by accrediting his work to Satan.

I was once asked what the initial sign of the baptism of the Holy Spirit was. I answered, "trouble". The pastor and his interpreter were totally confused as they hoped I would say tongues. I told them that everywhere Paul and the other apostles went under the power of the Holy Spirit there was trouble. People would get set free, healed, receive miracles and renounce all their evil practices. They loved the Holy Spirit. Other people would get upset as the status quo was shaken, business was lost, and they became protective of the wrong kingdom. They hated the moving of the Holy Spirit. Riots happened, people were beaten and imprisoned, churches were planted and their worlds were turned upside down. Be careful not to credit the works of God as the works of the evil one.

# MARK CHAPTER FOUR

# PART ONE

Jesus taught in parables. A comment in Strong's defines a parable as a narrative, fictitious but agreeable to the laws and usages of human life, by which either the duties of men or the things of God, particularly the nature and history of God's kingdom are figuratively portrayed[1]. A parable engages you in the learning process. You have to ponder the illustration for the truth and the application. It is a voyage of discovery and revelation. Once you get it you aren't likely to forget it.

---

[1] Strong's Concordance: Strong's number 3850
http://www.biblestudytools.com/lexicons/greek/kjv/parabole.html

I have always felt sorry for the people who weren't privileged to get the interpretation that the Twelve did. But if you notice in verse 10 it says the Twelve and the others around Him got His explanation. Jesus wasn't withholding revelation; He was looking for those who were willing to press into know more. Any teacher will tell you what a delight it is to teach students who want to learn. They draw the information out of you.

It seems harsh when you read, "The secret of the kingdom of God has been given to you. But to those on the outside everything is said in parables so that, '"they may be ever seeing but never perceiving, and ever hearing but never understanding; otherwise they might turn and be forgiven!"' One could almost think that there is an in-group and an out-group. One is privileged with understanding and the other is not privy to such access, hence, they will not be forgiven. Actually the scripture says if they did perceive and did understand they would turn, i.e., change their minds, and be forgiven. There is a need to look beyond the obvious to receive. Some people won't make the effort. They don't truly desire understanding.

Years ago a lady in our church shared her testimony of how she came to Christ. She had a yard sale which was attended by a man from the community that everyone knew had become "religious". It wasn't busy so she asked him why he became a Christian. He told her that was for him to know and her to find out. She was so upset that he wouldn't tell her that she set about finding out what he had that she didn't. It led to her meeting her Savior. Sometimes I think we answer questions that people aren't asking. Would we not be better to pique their curiosity instead of spoon-feeding them everything?

When I was first under the influence of the beckoning of the Holy Spirit, my in-laws said I must say a sinner's prayer to receive salvation. They never told me what the prayer was, so I read the bible through looking for this prayer. I remember finishing the bible and saying to Bonnie that I couldn't find it. "How was I ever going to get saved if I couldn't find the sinner's prayer?" But I had read enough to ask God to forgive me, to come into my heart and to confess Jesus before men so He would confess me before His Father and the angels. That statement kept me looking for a prayer that didn't exist but helped me receive revelation through the word that did lead to my salvation.

The kingdom of God is available to all that will seek

Him. Psalm 25:14 (Amp) states: "The secret of the sweet, satisfying companionship of the Lord have they who revere and worship Him, and He will show them His covenant and reveal to them its deep, inner meaning." On our 16$^{th}$ anniversary I arranged to have a yellow rose delivered to the door everyday for 16 days. The bell would ring, Bonnie would check to see who was there, and then find another rose. It took her several days to figure out the mystery of the yellow rose. But the joy it brought each day was so much more fun than giving them to her all at once. Each day she delighted in my love for her. How much more will we delight in the Lord's love as we discover all He has hidden for us?

# PART TWO

In verse 21 - 23 Jesus said to them, "Do you bring in a lamp to put it under a bowl or a bed? Instead, don't you put it on its stand? For whatever is hidden is meant to be disclosed, and whatever is concealed is meant to be brought out into the open. If anyone has ears to hear, let him hear." He used the illustration of a lamp to point out that the effectiveness of a parable is in what it discloses for those who are seeking. A lamp is useless if it is hidden. A parable is also useless if it's truth is left concealed. Everything that is concealed is to be brought out into the open. That's its purpose, just like a lamp's purpose is fulfilled in putting it upon a stand. He who has ears to hear let him pursue understanding. Revelation is not going to be simply dropped into our laps. We need to engage the Lord in seeking understanding.

I read once in a book on giving that every point of need that we had financially was intended as a point of fellowship with the Lord. The author felt that our need caused us to turn to the Lord and once again pursue Him. I think he is right. I think the purpose of parables is the same. The Lord has hidden truths so that we will engage Him in pursuing understanding. Human nature seems to ignore the Lord if all is going well and easy. We don't intend to, we just get too busy with the daily grind to notice our lack of fellowship.

Jesus then said: "Consider carefully what you hear," he continued. "With the measure you use, it will be measured to you--and even more. Whoever has will be given more; whoever does not have, even what he has will be taken from him." He is giving us a key to growing in our knowledge of God. Hearing – and how much you listen – determines the measure you receive. If you have understanding, you will be given more. If you don't pursue understanding, even what you do have will disappear. Our diligence to hear or understand the Lord determines how much we do receive.

I know people who envy the knowledge and wisdom of others. But the reason why the one has and the other doesn't is their priorities. One is in the word and pursuing the Lord for understanding, the envious one rarely pursues the word of God. Then they will say I just don't understand it when I read it. What they did have seems to be gone.

Parable in the Greek language also means to place side by side. You will find that there is a correlation in the parable of the sower with all the comments Jesus made about hearing. In all four cases the soil conditions reflected the condition of the heart. The heart is connected to faith. Romans 10:8 – 10 explains. "But what does it say? "The word is near you; it is in your mouth and in your heart," that is, the word of faith we are proclaiming: That if you confess with your mouth, "Jesus is Lord," and believe in your heart that God raised him from the dead, you will be saved. For it is with your heart that you believe and are justified, and it is with your mouth that you confess and are saved." Confession, which is essential to salvation, follows believing in your heart. Your heart is the seedbed of eternal life. Our heart must turn in repentance for us to believe. Romans 10:14 then states: 'And how can they believe in the one of whom they have not heard? And how can they hear without someone preaching to them?" Hearing is essential to releasing faith in the heart because Romans 10:17 states: "Consequently, faith comes from hearing the message, and the message is heard through the word of Christ." Faith, the currency of heaven, comes from hearing. If we want to grow in faith, we need to be careful how we hear for the measure that we use is the measure faith will come to us.

# PART THREE

**Mark 4:26 – 29: He also said, "This is what the kingdom of God is like. A man scatters seed on the ground. Night and day, whether he sleeps or gets up, the seed sprouts and grows, though he does not know how. All by itself the soil produces grain—first the stalk, then the head, then the full kernel in the head. As soon as the grain is ripe, he puts the sickle to it, because the harvest has come."**

In the introduction to this study of Mark the two themes that stood out are the kingdom of God and faith. In this parable Jesus reveals more of the nature of the kingdom of God. He says it is like a farmer planting his fields. He seeds the land then waits. He cannot make it grow.

The seed is representative of the word of God. Mark 16 says the disciples went out and preached everywhere, and the Lord worked with them and confirmed his word by the signs that accompanied it. No one questions the effectiveness of the early church in spreading the gospel, the good news of Jesus Christ. Even when persecution came upon the church as recorded in Acts it says the believers who fled Jerusalem preached the word wherever they went and the church grew. Paul says in Romans chapter 1 that he is not ashamed of the gospel because it is the power of God for the salvation of everyone who believes: first for the Jew, then for the Gentile. For in the gospel a righteousness from God is revealed, a righteousness that is by faith from first to last, just as it is written: "The righteous will live by faith." Our right standing with God is by faith, which comes from hearing the word of God.

In my experience and exposure to some of the church

in the west I think we have tried to analysis and dissect the growth process. We think by somehow understanding that process thoroughly we can release the kingdom of God in our cities and communities. The thinking seemed to be that the church was in decline, hence the need for intense study to produce a method that would reverse this trend. In essence we have done the same thing as scientists who have learned to clone a sheep. We are cloning churches in a hope to avert disaster and increase the kingdom.

Every growing church has been analyzed to find the reason for their expansion. We bypass the obvious in an attempt to unlock the secret to church growth. The disciples scattered seed in faith everywhere they went. That seed grew and produced a harvest.

For the kingdom of God to increase here on earth we need to preach the word of God in faith believing that it will do what it says it will. A seed has all this potential waiting for someone to plant it. You wouldn't plant it if you didn't think it would grow. We won't preach the word either if we don't think it will produce good results.

# PART FOUR

**Mark 4:30 – 32 Again he said, "What shall we say the kingdom of God is like, or what parable shall we use to describe it? It is like a mustard seed, which is the smallest seed you plant in the ground. Yet when planted, it grows and becomes the largest of all garden plants, with such big branches that the birds of the air can perch in its shade."**

The kingdom of God is like a mustard seed. Good things come in small packages. Never underestimate the power of small beginnings or the power of one person to change their world. Often we think what can I do? I'm only one on this staff of hundreds. What's the use?

The thing to remember is the potential that is within you. Colossians 2:9, 10 says: "For in Christ all the fullness of the Deity lives in bodily form, and you have been given fullness in Christ, who is the head over every power and authority". We have been given fullness through Christ. Within you and I as believers is the power and presence of the God who created the universe. When He spoke creation happened. That same power and goodness is within you. Just like a seed you are much more than what you appear to be. What is needed for that potential to be unlocked? Faith! Faith that God will work through you if you are willing!

Why compare the kingdom to a mustard seed? John Dominic Crossan points out that in Mediterranean climates, such as Galilee, black mustard is a managed weed. It would be obvious to state that the Kingdom of God is like the mighty Lebanon cedar, which also starts from a small seed, but instead Jesus says it's like the mustard weed.[2] Jewish law prohibited the planting of mustard in the garden. What was Jesus implying in the choice of this plant over others?

Weeds are a problem if left unchecked. They take over cultivated fields and gardens. Is the kingdom of God to spread like an unchecked weed? Have you ever observed how quickly they can spread? We planted a garden once but couldn't tell the weeds from the vegetables we had planted. By the time we could distinguish what was a weed and what wasn't, the weeds had totally dominated the garden. The kingdom left unchecked has the potential to take

---

[2] www.nationmaster.com/encyclopedia/Parable-of-the-Mustard-Seed

over. This was God's intent. The other thing we see is because it was good for oil and seasoning it was managed. Was Jesus also implying by this reference to a mustard seed that people would try to manage the growth of the kingdom of God and hold it in check?

Isn't that one of the things that is said when an outbreak of the Spirit of God happens as it did in the 90s? "It's out of control." "What's this unto?" "If it comes down, it must go out." "Everything must be done decently and in order." Revival seems to be stopped when men get it under control and in order.

## PART FIVE

At the end of the chapter Jesus is asleep in the stern of the boat when a furious squall comes up. The disciples in fear for their lives wake him. He rebuked the wind and the waves and the sea became calm. Then He said to his disciples, "Why are you so afraid? Do you still have no faith?" They were terrified and asked each other, "Who is this? Even the wind and the waves obey him!"

Faith is powerful. It is to quote my wife, Bonnie, the currency of heaven. Faith releases the power of God to act on our behalf. It is more than saving faith. It is kingdom faith. The kingdom of God is at hand to those who believe and act in faith. Faith can supersede natural laws and dynamics.

If we approach the kingdom of God within the limitations of laws of nature and science, we will limit the results of our faith. The disciples were experiencing the unchecked wildness of a fallen earth, something that many cultures have tried to appease through offerings to please the spirits behind these phenomena. In the boat they had the embodiment of the kingdom of God and His dominion over the whole earth. Kingdom against kingdom!

Jesus spoke and the earth became calm. His authority is unquestionable! He not only taught on the kingdom, he demonstrated the kingdom in action. His rebuke to them was revealing. One, they were afraid. Fear negates faith. Fear was the first thing that Adam said to God after he sinned. I hid because I was afraid. Fear left unchecked can block the effect of faith.

Even with some trepidation you can still press through in faith. It is much like not allowing a dog to see or sense your fear of them. If they sense it, you lose. If you control the fear, the animal will come under your authority.

Two, they were now terrified of Him. Are we not having these kinds of demonstrations of power because we are not overwhelmed by awe and reverence for our Lord? Do we underestimate our God because of our familiarity with Him? We think we know Jesus and how He will respond. We have pat answers like God is a gentleman who would not cause us to do something against our will. Ask King Saul if he felt treated gently when the Spirit came upon him and he prophesied day and night.

Our God is a not a toothless lion to be coddled but a wild lion to be revered.

# MARK CHAPTER FIVE

# PART ONE

The first 20 verses of this chapter deal with the account of the man with a legion of demons. This reads like some comic book superhero saga, the evil villain against the good guy. Possibly people see Jesus and his life on earth like a fictitious story of good against evil in a titanic battle to see who will win. But it is far from that. It is a real account of the kingdom of God meeting the kingdom of darkness. This man who had within him the power of at least 2000 demons when he came to Jesus could not resist His word. They fled! The book of James says for us to submit to God, resist the devil and he will flee. Flee means to run away in terror.

The narrative doesn't explain how he came to be this way just that he is. The number of demons within him was at least 2000 as this was the number of pigs that drowned. The added section titles in the bible call this the 'Healing of the demon-possessed Man'. The evidence is clear he was a demon-tormented man. There is nothing pretty about submitting yourself to the kingdom of Satan. He was wild, out of control, anti-social, isolated, crying out in pain and self-abusive with his cutting of himself. What a joy to be Satan's strong man!

Although the demons appeared to be in control, when he saw Jesus from a distance, he ran to Him and fell on his knees before Him. He saw hope and love in the form of a man, Jesus. The demons could not violate his will by stopping him from going to Jesus. No matter what the level of torment from demonic sources, if people see Jesus and want to go to Him, the demons cannot stop them. These scriptures give us a number of key truths for dealing with the demonic. **One is the willingness of people. If their will is willing, they will get set free.** They have to see their need for deliverance and be willing to send all their demonic friends packing. If they see comfort in them, they will not maintain their deliverance. They need to embrace Jesus.

Interestingly, the herders and the people from the town didn't want to embrace Jesus. You would assume after such an awesome display of God's power that they would be eager to hear more and be a part of God's kingdom. People may prefer to suffer with what they are familiar with rather than receive liberty and face the unknown. They didn't want the kingdom of God. Maybe they had already made that clear by breeding pigs contrary to the law of God. **It is another maxim that miracles do not always bring salvation to people.** Sometimes they prefer life the way it is, blinded by the lies of the evil one.

Surprisingly Jesus did not let the man come with them. He told him to go home to his family and tell them how much the Lord has done for him, and how He had mercy on the man. The man told everyone in the Decapolis region how much Jesus had done for him. Another key is sharing what Jesus has done for you with others. How He has set you free! **The power of your testimony will keep you and set others free.**

# PART TWO

There was "a woman who had been subject to

bleeding for 12 years. She had suffered a great deal under the care of many doctors and had spent all she had; yet instead of getting better she grew worse". This could be today not 2000 years ago. Many people still find this to be the case. As helpful and caring as the medical profession is there are cases that mystify them and they cannot seem to bring any resolution to them.

This healing has some interesting dynamics we need to catch. One, Jesus realized power had left him. Power left Him! Healing requires power as much as our salvation requires power. Paul says in I Corinthians that he came in a demonstration of God's power so that their faith would not rest upon man's word or wisdom but upon the power of God. And in Romans we are told that if the same Spirit that raised Christ from the dead dwells in you than that Spirit will quicken your mortal body. The whole process of salvation requires power. There is something tangible and real in our conversion and engagement with the kingdom of God.

Two, we need to note that not every attempt to touch Jesus draws the power required to bring healing or deliverance. Jesus was pressed on all sides by the crunch of people wanting to touch Him. When she touched His robe, He felt power depart from Him. We can touch Jesus but not draw what we need from Him. There must be more to healing prayer than words.

Three, we must understand that in the midst of the crowds with everyone pressing Him and touching Him only one person's touch drew power from Him. Why? His disciples were totally frustrated by His question as to who touched Him. But He was insistent in identifying the person. When she finally realized He wasn't going to be satisfied until He knew whom it was, she confessed. His response was not condemnation but commendation. He said, "Your faith has healed you." Faith released the power of God without Jesus even being aware of the need, desire or request. Faith is powerful.

Four, she pushed in where she was forbidden by Mosaic Law to be. Leviticus 15 speaks of the uncleanness of a woman having a discharge of blood and how any one who comes in contact with her becomes unclean. Jesus did not rebuke her for violating the law. Rather He commended her for her faith, told her to go in peace and be freed from her suffering. To touch Jesus sometimes you have to violate the conventional and accepted practices. The

Lord said mercy triumphs over justice.

# PART THREE

There are 3 events recorded in Mark 5. The first is dealing with the demoniac who is set free. The second is the woman with the issue of blood and the third is the death of Jairus' daughter. Each one is an example of the kingdom of God invading the territory of spiritual bondage Satan created.

The demoniac demonstrates freedom from tormenting evil spirits. The woman who was subject to bleeding shows the power of Jesus over sickness and disease. The Pharisee's daughter is the power of God over death. All 3 were loosed upon the earth through Adam's disobedience and have terrorized mankind ever since.

While Jesus was speaking with the woman of faith the news came that Jairus' daughter had died and there was no longer any reason to bother the teacher. Jesus told him not to be afraid; just believe. We need to manage fear. Fear eats away at faith based belief. If we allow our eyes or ears to dictate what we believe, then we will not see the kingdom of God. Fear when fully developed births unbelief and unbelief is the opposite of faith. Belief in Him can overcome sin, sickness and death.

When Jesus got to the house the mourning and grieving were in full swing. He tells them the child is not dead but asleep. They laughed and mocked Him for they all knew death when they saw it. This was a situation where anyone with common sense would know she is dead. Common sense is an enemy of God sense or faith. What we see as common is not of the kingdom of God. It is part of the corruption of the earth as a result of Adam's sin. We need God sense to move in the power of the Holy Spirit.

He said what He said because He had faith in God. Faith according to Hebrews 11:1 is being sure of what we hope for and certain of what we do not see. Jesus was sure that she was alive because He believed in faith. That faith was the evidence of what was not yet seen. When we have faith, we see things before they exist in the natural. The truth is what God says not what we see. We may see a dead body but what does God say? When my father had a massive heart attack the doctors said he was going to die that night. I prayed over him for healing. I did not have an immediate peace so I continued to pray in the Spirit. After 20 minutes I had peace and knew he would be ok. Within hours of that prayer they sent those of us who were in the waiting room home as he had stabilized. To see him the next day was remarkable. I knew before I saw.

Jesus knew this little girl was alive before He saw it. But He spoke out what He saw with faith not with His eyes. He also stopped Jairus from giving into fear that would undermine faith for what is in your heart is what you will speak out. If you have faith, you can speak of those who died as being alive. If you foster fear you will speak only death. The kingdom of God operates on faith.

# MARK CHAPTER SIX

# PART ONE

When Jesus returned to Nazareth (Mark 6:1-6) the people responded initially with amazement when he spoke. He obviously did some miracles initially as they commented on them. Their big problem was they knew Him after the flesh. They drew out the old labels: carpenter, Mary's son, and brother of. Then they took offence with Him. Why? Why would people be upset over His wisdom and miracles?

They were offended because of their familiarity. Jesus did not move into ministry until He was 30 as it was the appointed age for priests to begin ministry. He had 30 years to experience all of the life issues we encounter. No one will be able to say to Him, "you never faced what I faced". He did not go through life as the son of a wealthy or professional family. He was conceived in the minds of the people out of wedlock making Him the bastard son. He was not the pampered only child but one of more than 4 siblings. Suddenly He is the talk of the country. Now He was preaching to them incredible wisdom and doing miracles. Who did He think He was?

Paul says in 2 Corinthians 5:16, 17 "So from now on we regard no one from a worldly point of view. Though we once regarded Christ in this way, we do so no longer. Therefore, if anyone is in Christ, he is a new creation; the old has gone, the new has come!" Those who receive Christ are new creations. Their past is forgiven, their true destiny is released and they will act differently. We are not to regard them or ourselves in that old worldly way anymore.

The problem is those most familiar with us still see us that way. They struggle with the idea we could be different. Who are we to now preach the righteousness of Christ? We know who you are and what you did. In essence it is crab-ology. I understand that you only need a lid on a bucket to keep the first crab you catch in it. After you catch others they will pull the one on the verge of escape back in. Familiarity breeds contempt. The first convert to Christ in any family faces that contempt even long after many of the family become Christians.

It says in verse 6 "And he was amazed at their lack of faith". In light of the two themes throughout Mark of the kingdom of God and faith this incident is significant. Faith is crucial to the release of the power of God. Fear left unchecked will negate faith but familiarity also severely limits faith. Believers who have grown up surrounded by Christian influences are often inoculated against the power of the Holy Spirit. They may have heard it talked about but never demonstrated. They may have been told all the stories from the bible yet never experienced anything remotely close to the biblical accounts. They are familiar with a powerless, irrelevant Jesus! When the Spirit comes in power, they are often initially amazed, then offended. Their thinking towards Christ is worldly and unregenerate. They see Him only after the flesh. Truly this must be why Paul tells us in Romans 12 to be transformed by the renewing of our minds. Our thinking has to line up with the word of God for us to move in faith.

## PART TWO

**Verse 7, 12 and 13 "Calling the Twelve to him, he sent them out two by two and gave them authority over evil spirits.... They went out and preached that people should repent. They drove out many demons and anointed many sick people with oil and healed them."**

The twelve were sent out to do the same ministry that Jesus did. The present day church struggles with the whole manifestation of power and what levels of qualification do people need. They believe that the working of the Holy Spirit is only for believers and only within the confines of the Sunday service.

Yet the Lord Himself did not limit the moving of the Holy Spirit. In this passage His disciples were given authority over evil spirits. Authority in the Greek is exousia, which means the power of rule or government (the power of him whose will and commands must be submitted to by others and obeyed). This authority was not restricted to Jesus alone, or too believers of the risen Christ. These fellows didn't even know Jesus was going to be crucified, die, and rise from the dead. They were not born again through the spirit of God. They were ordinary Joes who were given delegated authority. In fact at one point in the Gospels James and John said to Jesus that they came across a man casting out demons in His name and they stopped him. Jesus said not to stop him that he was obviously for Him. All of this happened before His death and resurrection.

Do we as the church put a higher and more limiting criterion upon believers than Christ does? Why do we restrain our prayers and deliverance to church services or special meetings? People are looking for tangible demonstrations of the power of God. If we aren't seeing people delivered or healed outside the church or even in the church, who then is putting the limitations on the Holy Spirit?

What did they preach? They preached the message Jesus did that the kingdom of God was at hand. They preached repentance. They called people to change their minds about the kingdom of God. This was Jesus' message and it was theirs. Then they cast out demons and healed the sick. Both of these actions were explicit examples to the people of the power of the kingdom of God. They were also a key demonstration that helped to change people's minds.

## PART THREE

**Mark 6:14 "King Herod heard about this, for Jesus' name had become well known. Some were saying, "John the Baptist has been raised from the dead, and that is why miraculous powers are at work in him." 15 Others said, "He is Elijah." And still others claimed, "He is a prophet, like one of the prophets of long ago." 16 But when Herod heard this, he said, "John, the man I beheaded, has been raised from the dead!"'**

From verse 14 through 29 the final days of John the Baptist are recorded. The works of Jesus were becoming known throughout Israel by word of mouth, particularly after He had released His disciples to minister in the same authority. The tipping point had been reached. Enough people were talking about Him that it drew the attention of the ruling elite.

John had said when his disciples were upset over the numbers of people that were following Jesus that he must decrease while Jesus must increase. John was only the messenger preparing the way. He wasn't The Way. As I write this I wonder how often we who are called to serve the Lord forget we are just the messengers pointing the way to Jesus? Do we get caught up building our own ministry and it becomes all about us or do we stay true to being His witness?

The scriptures reveal the confusion in people's minds about who Jesus was. John the Baptist was prominent in creating the confusion. Herod even had partial revelation as to what was to come when he spoke of being raised from the dead. The confusion then as it is today is our propensity to want to find a label for everything that helps our understanding. The problem with this is we use old references for new phenomena. There was no one like Jesus before so how do you explain Him. But that puts us in our discomfort zone. We want to be able to explain everything so that we are in control. There is a general discomfort with mystery.

Verse 20 tells us that 'Herod feared John and protected him, knowing him to be a righteous and holy man. When Herod heard John, he was greatly puzzled; yet he liked to listen to him'. John was recognized as a righteous and holy man, yet he was beheaded. There is a cost in following the Lord. It is often said in evangelistic meetings that salvation doesn't cost you anything. Jesus paid the price; it's free. But He says 'as the master so the disciples'. The gospels are clear that only Jesus could fulfill the law and take away our sin. But they are also very clear that following Jesus will cost us everything. If we try to hold onto our life we will loose it. If we choose to give our life away we will gain it. I have heard believers say that God would never ask us to lose our lives like John did. In a sense that is syncretism where the truth of the faith is mixed with another belief system to come up with one that satisfies our desires and understanding. Verse 14 to 16 smelled of the initial stages of this.

Although Herod recognized John's holiness and liked to listen to him Herod still beheaded him to save face before his guests. No matter how much the world likes you or recognizes your holiness they are still fickle friends at best. If their self-interest is threatened you're dead. Until someone embraces the cross and accepts Christ's life they will have the capability of crucifying the Christ in you again and again. To see the kingdom of God come we need to be willing to lay down our lives.

# PART FOUR

**Mark 6:30 "The apostles gathered around Jesus**

**and reported to him all they had done and taught. 31 Then, because so many people were coming and going that they did not even have a chance to eat, he said to them, "Come with me by yourselves to a quiet place and get some rest." 32 So they went away by themselves in a boat to a solitary place"**


When the apostles returned from their ministry trip, they reported to Jesus all they had done. It is important after ministry to debrief. It gives you an opportunity to remember the wonderful things that God has done through you. It allows you to unpack any situations you didn't understand or feelings of attack. It strengthens your faith.


As humans we easily forget what happened to us, even if it is wonderful. Once at a meeting a friend came up for prayer for healing. I said that was no problem for the Lord had healed her of this weird disease the year before. She said what disease? She didn't remember until we talked about it. When she got the memory back, she was strengthened in her faith.


The Lord told the people of Israel to write a book of

remembrance and to tell their children what the Lord had done for them. They weren't a part of the exodus from Egypt or the time in the wilderness. But they needed to know the supernatural provision of the Lord then was available to them now. When Jehoshaphat was faced with the 3 nations coming up against Judah, he called all the people together and recounted all the great things God had done for them. It gave them courage, hope and faith to face what lay before them.

Jesus also took them away to a solitary place to get some rest. Ministry is physically draining. If we don't rest our bodies, we are vulnerable to the enemies attack. The spirit is willing but the flesh is weak. Temptation is strongest when our bodies are tired. Not only does temptation come to our eyes and our stomachs it comes to our sense of acceptance. Often when the doors for ministry open and people are flocking to us, we don't want to stop. What if it doesn't keep going? What if I take a week off, I may not get another opportunity.

Don't succumb to the temptation to go, go, go. Life in the Lord is a rhythm of rest, work, play and worship. Each one is essential to maintaining effective ministry.

# PART FIVE

**Mark 6:44 "The number of the men who had eaten was five thousand."**

When Jesus and the apostles landed in the solitary place there was a huge crowd waiting for them. Jesus had compassion on them for they were like sheep without a shepherd. The word compassion in the Greek means to be moved as to one's bowels, hence to be moved with compassion, have compassion (for the bowels were thought to be the seat of love and pity). This is not a colloquial phrase we would use now. Yet, when we are heartbroken or overwhelmed we will groan or feel things deeply in our abdomen. Don't let this escape you! Jesus, our Saviour, is moved with compassion for us. He is not indifferent or objective in His relationship to us. He feels deeply for us. One cannot feel this deeply and not respond. **Jesus will respond to us because He is moved by compassion. This too is the nature of the kingdom of God.**

So he taught them but instead of sending them away hungry he wanted to feed them. From 5 loaves and 2 fish He fed the crowd of 5000 plus for there were women and children accompanying the men. This is an outstanding miracle! But it wasn't Jesus alone. He said to His apostles, you feed them. When He had broken the bread and the fish and given thanks for them, he handed it to the disciples to distribute. They had 2 fish and 5 loaves split between the 12 of them. No matter what size the fish or loaves were, they were not going to feed 5000 to 10000 people. Can you imagine the trepidation the disciples felt, as they had to turn from their holy huddle around Jesus to face the hungry crowd? Once people have been promised something, whether they had any thought of it before or not, they expect it and can be very hostile if they don't get it. These men had to walk over to a group of 50 ravenous people with this bit of food and feed them. They probably thought, "Easy for you, Jesus, to say go feed them. You don't have to face them with this wee bit." The miracle didn't begin to happen until they handed a piece to the first person. The food either in their hand or in a basket was replaced so there was more to give. I can only imagine the joy that the apostles had when they saw that. They must have gone wild handing out food at that point. If they hadn't, why were there 12 large, full baskets left over? **That is another wonderful truth about God. He doesn't scrimp and only give just enough. He is excessive in His giving.**

Again and again throughout Mark's Gospel we are given examples of divine intervention over the material world. The laws of nature are consistent and constant but they can be overruled by the nature of the kingdom of God. What is impossible for man is possible for God! **He is willing to do the impossible through us as He did with His first apostles. What do we expect and have faith for?**

# PART SIX

**Mark 6:48 – 50 "He saw the disciples straining at the oars, because the wind was against them. About the fourth watch of the night he went out to them, walking on the lake. He was about to pass by them, but when they saw him walking on the lake, they thought he was a ghost. They cried out, because they all saw him and were terrified"**

Jesus had sent the people away and the disciples off in their boats so He could pray. In the early morning hours He walks across the lake and appears to be going to pass right by the disciple's boat. The man was walking on water! What? As I said before the Gospel of Mark is full of phenomenon that are incredible.

Doesn't that excite you? I love that I have a God who is so much more than what this world contains. He is not bound by the limitations of the natural laws that seem to govern earth. I love knowing that He can do way above and beyond what I dare think or ask. He is supernatural.

The amazing thing is Jesus was fully man and did not draw on His deity to walk on the water or to feed 5000 with 5 loaves and 2 fish. He ministered through the baptism in the Holy Spirit. We have that same Holy Spirit available to us. When we ask for the Holy Spirit to come upon us, we don't get the junior version or the restricted version. We get the fullness of the Holy Spirit. We have the potential to feed the thousands and to walk on water too.

The kingdom of God is not anemic but powerful and mighty. Every miracle and supernatural event that Jesus performed is more evidence of the kingdom of God. Jesus' message was repent for the kingdom of God is at hand. Then He demonstrated it so that people could believe. The kingdom was at hand for where the King is there is the kingdom. We who believe have the king living within us through the

Holy Spirit. We represent the kingdom of God on earth. We can believe that the same power that worked through Jesus will work through us.

The key is not our need but our faith. The kingdom of God comes to those who believe.

## PART SEVEN

**Mark 6:54 – 56 "As soon as they got out of the boat, people recognized Jesus. They ran throughout that whole region and carried the sick on mats to wherever they heard he was. And wherever he went--into villages, towns or countryside--they placed the sick in the marketplaces. They begged him to let them touch even the edge of his cloak, and all who touched him were healed."**

When Jesus shows up, people respond. It's the same today in church. The church can pursue all different types of methods to attract people to the church. But the most effective method is to have Jesus show up. When the power of God comes people get excited.

These people had an expectation that Jesus would heal the sick. Expectation is vital to releasing the power of faith. You get what you expect. It is amazing to see the difference between conferences and Sunday services. People who go to conferences are looking for something to happen. They all come together with an expectancy of the presence of God. Most Sunday morning services don't have that level of anticipation. People simply seem to go through the motions when it comes to normal services. Then they wonder why God doesn't show up and do miracles in their midst.

Jesus didn't stop and pray for these people. Their faith was so high all they needed for healing was to touch the edge of His cloak. What a difference attitude makes! Think about the people in Nazareth and the people from this region. One didn't receive because of their familiarity; the other did because of their expectation.

The healings all happened in the marketplace. As my dear wife says this is the first example of marketplace ministry. The Holy Spirit is not restricted to a building. He will touch people wherever they are.

Jesus went to where the people were. Equally the people pursued Him wherever they heard He was. Both coming together creates amazing results.

# MARK CHAPTER SEVEN

# PART ONE

**Mark 7:20 "What comes out of a man is what makes him unclean"**

The first 23 verses of chapter 7 are an account of another conflict with the Pharisees and the teachers of the law. They were deeply offended that Jesus' disciples were eating with unwashed hands. It violated all their traditions and sacred practices. Jesus quotes Isaiah in rebuking their position. He chastens them for traditions of men that prohibit the Law of Moses from being applied. Ultimately He tells them that they have nullified the principles of God by their regulations.

Then He goes on to explain that it isn't what you eat that defiles you but what comes out of your heart. The things we say defile us. Our conversation reveals the condition of our heart. If we listen closely to what we say, it's like having a mirror placed in front of us. We get to see what is within our heart.

This situation is a classic example of the subtlety of Satan's kingdom infiltrating what was originally God's kingdom. Religion makes up laws that have nothing to do with the will of God. As good as the intention was to create a buffer zone around God's law so there wouldn't be any possibility of violating the law these traditions and addendums then became the practices they so fervently enforced. There was no life in them for they weren't from God. Jesus constantly violated the practices that were not laws from God.

One system focuses on the external, the other, the kingdom of God, focuses on the heart issues. The religious system allows people to appear righteous while running amok in their attitudes. This is why unbelievers can stand and point a finger at believers because they see such hypocrisy between Christians' actions and their attitudes. We will fervently defend our traditions and practices today at the cost of ignoring Jesus' commandments. We will shut down the moving of the Holy Spirit because we don't do that in our church. We will make a ritual out of attending church twice on Sunday to the neglect of our family or our actual spiritual growth.


Have you ever wondered why well known famous men and women of God can have huge moral failures while representing the Body of Christ from the pulpit, or to the media, or within government lobbies? What happened to them? They started to live in the form without the spirit. They started to maintain the appearance of righteousness while having unchecked heart issues.


One kingdom is all practices and traditions that burden, bind and blind believers. The kingdom of God sets us free of our burdens, bondages and blindness. With that freedom comes an accountability to be aware of that which can defile us and to deal with it appropriately. The kingdom of God does not suffer religion lightly.

# PART TWO

**Mark 7:28 "Yes, Lord," she replied, "but even the dogs under the table eat the children's crumbs."**

Jesus and his team had left the country to get some rest. He really didn't want anyone to know He was there. Rest is very important to sustaining ministry. Jesus drew away numerous times to find refreshing and rest. On occasion He still ended up ministering but these were the exception not the rule. Often when the opportunities to minister open up to people they run from one event to the next without any breaks for fear the door of opportunity may swing close. This would be great if we were spirit only but we have been put in bodies with physical limitations. Weariness has two effects: one, we end up serving out of an empty well and two, we are more prone to succumb to temptation when we are weary.

You may think you are getting away with ministering from the empty well but believe me people know when your resources are slim. They can feel the tiredness in the spirit. At our college we had a speaker who was so tired from all the irons he had in the fire that it was contagious. The whole class could barely stay awake during his lectures. Like the prodigal son, when all the Father's resources are gone, people leave. It's not you they want, it's the life of Jesus flowing in you that draws them.

The resistance to temptation is least when we are bone weary. The disciples in the Garden of Gethsemane could not stay awake to pray with Jesus for even an hour. Sleep overcame them. Jesus said the spirit is willing but the flesh is weak. God, himself, worked 6 days and rested on the $7^{th}$. Jesus said the Sabbath was made for man not man for the Sabbath. We need rest to be restored. Adrenalin can look like anointing but it won't last.

A Greek woman approached Jesus at this time that wanted Jesus to deliver her daughter of a demon. He was resistant as His primary mission was to invite the Jews as God's chosen instruments into a new release of the kingdom of God. She was not deterred by his rebuff. The Jews called the Gentiles dogs but she wasn't fazed by this insult. She persevered and was rewarded for her quick thinking. She called forth the promises of God before their time for God always intended all people to be included in His kingdom. Israel was to be His ambassadors of His kingdom inviting people to receive His grace. He has called all believers through Jesus to be His ambassadors to minister reconciliation with God and open the door to His kingdom.

Lastly, distance or a person's presence does not limit faith's effectiveness. The child was set free at home while her mother was with Jesus. To see healing and deliverance we don't always have to be close and laying on hands to see them set free. Calling on Jesus in faith will move the hand of God despite the distance. According to our faith be it unto us.

# PART THREE

**Mark 7:37 "He has done everything well, " they said. " He even makes the deaf hear and the mute speak."**

When Jesus returned to the region of the Decapolis from His Holydays, some people brought a man to be healed from deafness. Jesus put his fingers in his ears, spit, touched the man's tongue, and then said, "Be open!" Instantly the man could hear and speak. Notice that Jesus did not pray to God and ask Him to heal the man. Jesus touched the places of affliction and then commanded them to respond to His word. As unusual and odd as it feels, if we want to see people healed, we need to realize we may have to command body parts to be healed. We need to touch the body and command it to obey. Talking to God is lovely but the Spirit is waiting for you to speak the word.

Jesus was the word with God and was God from the beginning. John 1:3 says, "Through him all things were made; without him nothing was made that has been made." Jesus created the human body through speaking the word. It still responds to the word of God. It may seem really odd or you may feel embarrassed to speak to someone's body but if you want to see healing happen it often requires we speak to the body to be healed.

Jesus took the man aside from the crowd as his actions could be mocked and hinder the healing. We need to be sensitive to the leading of the Holy Spirit. As the Spirit leads respond. If He prompts you to put your fingers in someone's ears, do it. If He says draw them aside, do it. Our effectiveness is really contingent on our obedience to the Spirit of the Lord.

# MARK CHAPTER EIGHT

# PART ONE

**Mark 8:11** "The Pharisees came and began to question Jesus. To test him, they asked him for a sign from heaven. He sighed deeply…"

In the verses prior to verse 11 Jesus had spent 3 days teaching the people. They had nothing left to eat. Out of compassion for the people Jesus wanted to feed them. The disciples really missed the plot. Where are we going to get food in this remote place was their question. Jesus always asks what do we have. It only takes a little for the Lord to perform miracles.

They had 7 loaves of bread. The number 7 represents complete. Seven loaves was enough to complete the job of feeding 4000 men plus women and children. As with the feeding of the 5000 Jesus broke the bread and the few fish and gave it to the disciples to distribute. The people ate and were satisfied. The disciples picked up 7 basketfuls of leftovers. This speaks volumes. When they did it the first time with feeding the 5000, their enthusiasm resulted in 12 basketfuls left. This time there was only 7.

What happened to their enthusiasm? It appears as though they were a little more complacent this time around. How can we get complacent over the miraculous? Jesus then encounters the Pharisees who ask for a sign from heaven. Why does this generation ask for a miraculous sign? All around them signs and wonders were happening and yet they couldn't see them. No sign would be given to them because they wouldn't have seen it. Their hearts were hard.

Jesus in Matthew 5 said, "Blessed are the pure in heart, for they will see God." To see God we need a heart massage, a softening of the heart. There are none so blind as the religious who think they have all the answers. God responds to those who are seeking, who don't have all the answers any longer. We truly need a gift of repentance, the ability to change our mind, to see the kingdom of God.


When the apostle Paul was struck blind on the road to Damascus he thought he was protecting the kingdom of God. Instead Jesus told him he was prosecuting the kingdom. When Ananias prayed for Paul, something like scales fell from his eyes and he could see again. Paul describes in Philippians 3 what he was like before Jesus revealed himself to him. He says, "…in regard to the law, a Pharisee; as for zeal, persecuting the church, as for legalistic righteousness, faultless."


Even today the church calls for miracles while ignoring those happening all around them. Invitations to meetings with signs and wonders are ignored. Is this why we are told to have faith like little children? Have you seen children grow tired of reading the same book or watching the same video over and over again? They never tire of a good story. They enjoy it and appreciate the marvel of it. Oh, to have hearts like little children when it comes to the kingdom of God.

# PART TWO

**Mark 8:15 "Be careful," Jesus warned them. "Watch out for the yeast of the Pharisees and that of Herod."**

Throughout this study of Mark the themes of the kingdom of God and faith infiltrate virtually every episode. Each encounter with the Pharisees is a clash of kingdoms. Jesus warns His disciples to beware of the yeast of the Pharisees and of Herod. We need to be equally as aware today of this yeast.

The Pharisees represent the religious kingdoms of this earth. Paul warned the Galatians about this. He asked who had so easily bewitched them. Having started with grace, how could they have gone back to works? Many people receive a revelation of Jesus Christ as their savior. His sacrifice makes us right with God. We on our own will never ever come close to pleasing the righteous requirements of the law. All our attempts will be fruitless and in vain. Only through His life, death and resurrection can we be right with God and truly whole again. It is amazing how little yeast from the religious system is required to contaminate our thinking. Just as yeast flourishes and multiplies in warm, moist flour so does religious thinking in the midst of people getting a little on fire for God. Whoosh! It spreads. People with supposedly no religious background or experience manifest religious works as quickly as those who have spent their whole life in churches. They become convinced that sinners are untouchable, church buildings are the only place to be saved, or they must read their word and pray every night before they sleep or the Lord will leave them as unworthy when He returns. It becomes performance orientation, trying to please and win God's favor when you already have it.

The yeast of Herod is mixing worldly ways into the kingdom of God. Herod represented the world, the pride of men, the lust of their eyes and the desire for power. At the end of this chapter after Peter has had the revelation that Jesus is the Christ the son of the Living God he precedes to chasten the Lord for sharing of His death and resurrection. In verse 33 when Jesus turned and looked at his disciples, he rebuked Peter. "Get behind me, Satan!" he said. "You do not have in mind the things of God, but the things of men." He looked at His other disciples before He rebuked Peter for He knew if this were left unchecked they would be infected too.

The church is not an earthly kingdom. It is not about power, wealth and gain. It is about sacrifice, sharing and giving. The yeast of Herod brings the fear and nakedness of the Garden into every present situation. I am naked, alone and need protection. I must take care of myself, secure my future, own my house and have pensions and investments to cover me. How can I trust God to provide? How can I risk all in faith for a greater kingdom? Can I trust Him? The yeast infiltrates the church, the people of God, who are to bring the goodness of His kingdom to their neighbors. When I have my nest egg in place, then I'll give out of my excess. If you don't give with the little you have, you will never be free to give out of your abundance. You won't know God's provision and blessing is real. It will only be words you give lip service to. A great way to experience God's goodness to us is to give when we don't think we have enough. He never fails us but you will only truly know this by trusting Him and obeying His word. We miss so much when we allow the yeast of the Pharisees and of Herod to contaminate us.

# PART THREE

**Mark 8:22 - 26 "They came to Bethsaida, and some people brought a blind man and begged**

**Jesus to touch him. He took the blind man by the hand and led him outside the village. When he had spit on the man's eyes and put his hands on him, Jesus asked, "Do you see anything?" He looked up and said, "I see people; they look like trees walking around." Once more Jesus put his hands on the man's eyes. Then his eyes were opened, his sight was restored, and he saw everything clearly. Jesus sent him home, saying, "Don't go into the village."''**

There are three things that jump out with the healing of this man. One, why did Jesus take him out of the village of Bethsaida? In Matthew and Luke Jesus denounced the cities in which most of His miracles were done including Bethsaida. He said it would not bode well for them in the judgment. Cities like Sodom would have repented if the miracles had been done there. There is a Day of Judgment coming. We who have named the name of Jesus do not have to fear it. Because of God's mercy and longsuffering He has not hastened it but it will come. It is a shame that people mistake His grace to them as there being no God. Jesus took the man out of the village because their hearts were hard and unrepentant. There is definitely a time of grace and then it is withdrawn. Miracles do not guarantee a repentant heart or changed life. If you need a miracle you may have to go to a location where the atmosphere is one of true repentance. There seem to be cities or nations where historically there has been more of an open heaven regarding healings and miracles. These locations have been known for their numerous revivals where other places have never had one.

Two, the man had obviously been able to see at one time in his life. He could identify that people looked like trees. If he had always been blind he wouldn't have known the difference. There is great hope that if you once possessed something and then lost it, it is not lost forever. The Lord can return to you what injury, age, sickness or disease has stolen from you. In Jesus there is always hope!

The third thing is Jesus prayed twice for the same healing. There is teaching that says you only pray once for something and that is it. To pray again is to negate your faith. But Jesus, the Son of God, prayed, asked how it was and then prayed again. Healing can happen in stages. We can put such high expectations that it must happen instantly the first time that we fail to appreciate the first stage of a healing. As believers we shouldn't be afraid to ask people we are praying for what is happening to them. Their feedback allows us to pray with more accuracy. Persistence pays off in the kingdom of God.

# PART FOUR

**Mark 8:29 "But what about you?" he asked. "Who do you say I am?" Peter answered, "You are the Christ."**

When Peter spoke this forth, the gospel of Matthew tells us that Jesus commended him for the revelation. Jesus also said that this revelation was not of his or any man's doing but by the revelation of His Father in heaven. It has to be revelation for up to this time they were astounded again and again by the things that Jesus could do. He stilled the wind, calmed the sea, fed 5000 plus and 4000 plus with next to nothing yet they didn't really understand who He was. No one really does without revelation.

Jesus says no one has seen the Father except the son and whom He reveals the Father to. John 6:44 "No one can come to me unless the Father who sent me draws him, and I will raise him up at the last day". There is a drawing of people to Jesus that is the work of the Father. The Father opens their eyes to see

Jesus as the way to eternal life. But there is also the role of Jesus in revealing the Father as well. In John 14:6 Jesus answered, "I am the way and the truth and the life. No one comes to the Father except through me." To get to the Father we must come through Jesus, there is no other way. But to come through Jesus we need that inspirational revelation to see Him.

I used to share my testimony with people who could not understand what I was saying. To me it was so clear, yet to them it was completely beyond them. I would tell them of the presence of Jesus in my room as I read the bible. They think you are daft until the light comes on. As believers we need to pray for people to have revelation from God. Without it they are blind and can't see the truth. The disciples are classic examples of being with Jesus but not understanding who He was.

Years ago I had a man in the church whose boredom with the whole service and my message kept me humble. One Sunday I met him before the service and he was glowing with excitement and new life. He told me that he had been to a country and western gospel concert the night before and had responded to the call to give his life to Jesus. He was born again and truly excited. I was thankful and amazed that anyone could get saved through country and western but it was the medium through which God revealed Jesus to him.

Blessed are we to whom the Father has revealed the Son. Without this revelation we can't see the kingdom of God.

# PART FIVE

**Mark 8:34, 35 "If anyone would come after me, he must deny himself and take up his cross and follow me. For whoever wants to save his life will lose it, but whoever loses his life for me and for the gospel will save it."**

Every nation that has armed forces has a motto and a code of honor, which the recruits commit to upon enlisting. In times of war it is quite clear that you are prepared to give up your life to protect your country and all that it stands for. Liberty and freedom have come to many nations of the world through a very high cost in human lives. We have days to commemorate those who gave the ultimate sacrifice so our country could be free. There is much scorn for those who appear not to recognize the sacrifice.

How much more should we be willing to lay down our lives for the freedom of those held in bondage under a cruel and evil kingdom? History tells us of the high price saints of old paid for their allegiance to the kingdom of God. As they paid the price more and more believers were added to their numbers. The church has grown immensely during these times of direct warfare and persecution.

Jesus is our supreme commander and chief. He leads by example. Jesus asks no less from us than what He gave. He went to the cross for us so that we could be free. We must be prepared to lay down our lives daily whether we ever face martyrdom or not. To say the Gospel is free is untrue. We couldn't meet the demands of the Law but Christ did. He made what was impossible for man possible. Our restoration to God calls us not to work to maintain our salvation but to give our lives for that citizenship which we received in the kingdom of God. Through the life of the Holy Spirit within us we have the power to forsake our kingdom to pursue His kingdom.

In the kingdom of God the army of Christ has a motto: Take Up Your Cross and Follow Me.

# MARK CHAPTER NINE

# PART ONE

**Mark 9:1 And he said to them, "I tell you the truth, some who are standing here will not taste death before they see the kingdom of God come with power."**

The church often seems to be locked into one of two positions regarding the kingdom of God. They either talk about the kingdom of God and its influence in the past or they talk about one day the kingdom of God will come to earth. Past or future, but Jesus was not talking about the past or the far-flung future. He was talking of it within their lifetime.

This habit of talking about the kingdom historically is not only referring to the days of Jesus and the apostles. There are people who once encountered an experience with the kingdom of God through the power of the Holy Spirit. These people may have been with a new church birthed out of the Charismatic movement of the 70s. There was a reality of His kingdom coming on earth as it was in heaven at that time for those people. When things started to happen spiritually in 1994 some of these people would say I remember being touched once like this back in 1974. The kingdom had become a bygone experience. They were godly people who lived on the memories of what had happened once through the kingdom. Faithful but not expectant!

There are churches that are always looking for the return of Christ and His ushering in the kingdom of God. In the early 80s some church organizations were living with the expectancy that Christ would return within 5 years. There was a book written called '88 Reasons Why Christ Would Return in 1988'. Twenty-five years later the return of Christ hasn't happened. Expectant but disappointed!

Jesus said to His disciples within their lifetime they would see the kingdom of God coming in power. Three of them, John, James and Peter, experienced the transfiguration of Christ on the mountain. He was so surrounded by the power and presence of God that He glowed. Was this what Jesus meant? It was a sample of the intensity of the presence of God and something we could believe for. But He does say a number of times be it unto you according to your faith. John introduced Jesus as the one who would baptize in power. Jesus was talking about the outpouring of the Holy Spirit on Pentecost. This was the beginning of the kingdom of God being within us.

The kingdom of God became accessible to all believers through the sacrifice of Christ. The resurrected Jesus told His disciples to wait in Jerusalem until they received power to be His witnesses unto the ends of the earth. On Pentecost the Spirit came. The kingdom was and will be on earth, but it is present now.

## PART TWO

Verses 1 through 10 describe action on the Mount of

Transfiguration. As the four of them were on top of the mountain Jesus was transfigured before them. Strong's has two definitions of the Greek word. One is Jesus was basically aglow with divine light. The other says to change form. After that happened Elijah and Moses appeared. Whatever happened on that mountain must have been quite spectacular. Peter, James and John were very frightened.

Could Jesus have transformed into His immortal form as He was without sin? When He was resurrected and talking to His disciples on the Emmaus Road, they didn't recognize Him. Neither did Mary in the garden after His resurrection. She initially thought He was the gardener. I am sure He did radiate a divine light when it was over as Moses did when he returned from the mountain after 40 days with the Lord.

This event happened after Peter shared the revelation that Jesus was the Christ, the Son of the Living God. So why Moses and Elijah of all the historic figures in Israel's past? Why not David and Elisha or Daniel?

These two men were very significant in establishing the kingdom of Israel. Moses led the people out of captivity in Egypt. He gave them the Law of God that established the moral and ethical basis of their society. He gave them the guidelines to have a just and equitable society that rightly represented the kingdom of God.

Elijah was the prophet who confronted Ahab, the son of Omri. I Kings 16:30 tells us that Ahab did more evil in the eyes of the Lord than any kings before him. Not only did he commit the sins of Jeroboam he also through his marriage to Jezebel began to serve Baal and worship him. He led the nation into more and more idolatry. Elijah brought spiritual and governmental restoration back to Israel. He destroyed the prophets of Baal and proved to the people that there was only one God of Israel. To this day the Jewish people set a cup for Elijah at their Seder meals. They expect him to return proclaiming the coming of the Messiah.

The two of them represent the Law and the Spirit. Jesus said in John 4 that God was seeking believers who would worship Him in spirit and in truth. The kingdom of God as established through Jesus is to reflect both the Spirit and truth.

The transfiguration gives us a glimpse into the possibilities of the kingdom here on earth. It also affirmed Jesus and gave Him strength to go forward. From this point on He talked to His disciples about His impending suffering, death and resurrection from the dead. They didn't understand what He was telling them as they were expecting a kingdom like all the others here on earth. They needed to see the difference even if they didn't understand. Later they could say, 'this is that'.

# PART THREE

**Mark 9:23, 24   "'If you can'?" said Jesus. "Everything is possible for him who believes." Immediately the boy's father exclaimed, "I do believe; help me overcome my unbelief!"**

Verse 14 through 29 of Mark 9 covers the incident with the boy who had a spirit from birth that would throw him into the fire or the water to destroy him. His father brought him to the disciples to heal him but they were unable to cast the demon out. When Jesus arrived the disciples were arguing with the teachers of the law.

There is a tendency when we are ineffective in the things of the kingdom to theologically try to justify our ineptitude. When Jesus asked what they were arguing about the boy's father explained his request. Jesus response was 'O, unbelieving generation'. Rather than argue or try to defend yourself when healings or miracles don't happen, we need to grow in faith. This man said to Jesus if you can. Jesus' response was everything is possible for him who believes. The father said he did believe but asked for help to overcome his unbelief.

We all have levels of unbelief. We may believe Jesus can save us but not heal us. We may believe the Holy Spirit used to do miracles but doesn't today. We may believe that Jesus acts on behalf of others but not for us. Unbelief is the opposite of faith. Jesus could do very little in Nazareth because of their unbelief.

So, how do we overcome our unbelief? For this man it was Jesus delivering his son that dealt with his unbelief. Our faith will grow when we see the kingdom of God in action. I was an unbeliever until I saw my father-in-law healed. My position on God up till then was if He were real He would do the same things today that were done in the days of Jesus. When a miracle happened to a credible person, I was faced with the reality of who God is and what will I do with His claims? It led me to believing in Jesus Christ through faith. Because he was healed I believed that God could heal. When I didn't see that many healings I went to a bible college that had supernatural healings. There my faith increased again.

If the kingdom of God is activated here on earth through faith, then wouldn't the kingdom of darkness promote anything that would cause unbelief? If theories and philosophies can cause doubt, which will lead to unbelief, then it would be the ideal weapon against the kingdom of God. When the disciples asked why they couldn't cast out the demon, Jesus told them that it only came out through prayer. They argued with the teachers instead of connecting with God through prayer. The source of our faith is in God not in our theology.

# PART FOUR

**Mark 9: 34 - 35 But they kept quiet because on the way they had argued about who was the greatest. Sitting down, Jesus called the Twelve**

**and said, "If anyone wants to be first, he must be the very last, and the servant of all."**


Jesus was trying to teach His disciples about His death and resurrection but they didn't get it. They were afraid to ask Him because it wasn't the first time He had mentioned it. He then asked them what they had been arguing about. They were quiet as they didn't want to confess that it was about who amongst them would be the greatest.


Their thinking was the thinking of this world system. Who will be the greatest?

We would call this common sense. Surely someone has to be the leader and the most gifted of the group. A body with two heads is a freak so someone has to be the successor and obviously the one who is greatest is the likely candidate. This worldly thinking is contrary to kingdom of God thinking and at enmity with it. The sinful mind is hostile to God and opposes Him.


This mind set says our ambition is to be the best at whatever we do. To be first means we will have favored positions and status. People will serve us and admire us. We will have the most money and access to all that wealth can buy. One can see this thinking by observing the lavish embassies that are found in capital cities. They are big and ostentatious.

Jesus spends the last 20 verses of chapter 9 explaining a different attitude that would lead to greatness in the kingdom of God. He says if you want to be first, you must be the very last and servant of all. Talk about turning things upside down. He talks about our attitude being one that welcome little children, for in many cultures the children are the least honored. So we should give honor to those who have been ignored and despised. We need to accept others who act in the name of Jesus but are not in our personal group. These people may not be with us but if they do a miracle in His name they aren't in opposition to Him.

Then he talks about kindness. If we willingly give a cup of water in His name, then we will not lose our reward. The world says hold everything to yourself; share only when you have established your own security. All of which leads to miserliness, the exact opposite of our heavenly Father.

He emphasized not causing little ones to stumble and sin. These may include people who are adults but have only recently come to faith. Our attitudes can cause them to do things they don't have faith for yet. We need to be aware of our own capability to sin, and to deal with it. We are also the salt of the world. We add the flavor of God in the world and preserve it through mercy and peace with one another.

This type of thinking reflects the kingdom of God. It is a position of humility, not arrogance. We can recognize our own limitations and yet still respond in kindness and generosity.

# MARK CHAPTER TEN

# PART ONE

**Mark 10:2 - 3 "Some Pharisees came and tested him by asking, "Is it lawful for a man to divorce his wife?" "What did Moses command you?" he replied."**

In the first 12 verses of the chapter Jesus is teaching when the Pharisees test Him with a question about divorce. The Pharisees were always testing Jesus with matters of the Law to see if they could catch Him in error to discredit Him. They saw Him drawing crowds of people and liberating them with His teachings and His deeds. Their position of leadership was threatened. It is amazing that they who hated the

Roman domination would fight so hard to preserve the status quo. Instead of embracing the Christ they crucified Him to maintain their positions.

Jesus turned their question back upon them. What did Moses say? He would fight law with law. They said that Moses permitted divorce. Jesus said it was due to the hardness of their heart that Moses wrote this law. Hardness of heart comes from abiding in sin. Hebrews 3: 13 states: "But encourage one another daily, as long as it is called Today, so that none of you may be hardened by sin's deceitfulness".

Jesus then tells the Pharisees in verses 6 – 9 "But at the beginning of creation God 'made them male and female.' 'For this reason a man will leave his father and mother and be united to his wife, and the two will become one flesh.' So they are no longer two, but one. Therefore what God has joined together, let man not separate." God's plan was for a man and a woman to live together as one. Unfortunately Adam sinned and released sin's consequences upon all mankind. Sin hardens the heart. Just as it brought separation between God and man it can bring separation between husbands and wives, brothers, family and friends.

Jesus endorses His Father's ideal. He also knows that no one is capable of fulfilling the Law and as a result we sin. This bondage of sin is what He came to set us free from. Hebrews 4:15 - 16 "For we do not have a high priest who is unable to sympathize with our weaknesses, but we have one who has been tempted in every way, just as we are--yet was without sin. Let us then approach the throne of grace with confidence, so that we may receive mercy and find grace to help us in our time of need."

# PART TWO

**Mark 10:14 – 15 "Let the little children come to me, and do not hinder them, for the kingdom of God belongs to such as these. I tell you the truth, anyone who will not receive the kingdom of God like a little child will never enter it."**

Remembering that the main themes of Mark that we are looking at in this study are faith and the Kingdom of God we have two incidents layered almost on top of each other. The first is His receiving the little children and the second is the rich young man who asked what he must do to inherit eternal life.


Jesus rebuked His disciples when they were stopping the little children being brought to Him. He said we must receive the kingdom of God like little children to enter it. What is the key within little children?


A little child is dependent on their parents. They don't have any ambition or need for wealth. They haven't had any experiences that make them cynical nor have they had enough opportunities to sin, which hardens one's heart. They look to their parents to provide all that they need. They have complete confidence in their parents' care and protection. Generally speaking they are not thinking about where their next meal is coming from. Children from good homes don't have a concern or care for their wellbeing. This is the same attitude that we need to have to enter the kingdom of God. We need to relax in the loving care and arms of our heavenly Father.


Jesus then meets a man who has done everything right according to the Law. Mark 10:21, 22: "Jesus looked at him and loved him. "One thing you lack," he said. "Go, sell everything you have and give to the poor, and you will have treasure in heaven. Then come, follow me." At this the man's face fell. He went away sad, because he had great wealth." Note two things, one, Jesus loved him and yet said he lacked one thing to inherit eternal life. He needed to sell everything and give it to the poor. Then follow Him. That seems like a huge cost considering he was very wealthy. But the second thing was that the young man couldn't do it. The wealth owned him not the other way around. His dependency was in his wealth not in Jesus. Unlike a little child who would have no idea what the money meant this young man couldn't give it up. Jesus said how hard it is for the rich to enter the kingdom of God.

Peter says we gave up everything to follow you to which Jesus said anyone who does will receive a hundred times back in this lifetime plus persecutions and eternal life. The young man did not wait long enough to hear what his sacrifice would have done for him. If he had given it all away, he would have received the eternal life he was looking for, plus many times more than he gave returned in his lifetime. Once you have given all for Jesus sake and the gospel you aren't as concerned about the return. You become like little children – carefree and resting in the arms of your heavenly Father.

# PART THREE

**Mark 10:41 "When the ten heard about this, they became indignant with James and John."**

Jesus again was teaching His disciples about what was going to happen to Him in the near future. Ever since Peter had the revelation that Jesus was the Christ, the son of the Living God, Jesus had talked to them plainly about His impending suffering, death and resurrection. They just didn't understand it.

Immediately after sharing it once again James and John asked Him if they could be seated one on the right and one on the left in His glory. They were looking for the most imminent positions of power in His kingdom. The others were incensed when they heard about it because they wanted those positions. These men were not driven by their desire to lay down their lives for mankind. They wanted power, prestige and wealth.

Jesus takes the opportunity to teach them about true kingdom of God leadership. You mustn't lord it over people like the gentile rulers do. If you want to be first you must be a slave or servant to all. "For even the Son of Man did not come to be served, but to serve, and to give his life as a ransom for many." Jesus sets the benchmark for leadership with this statement. Sorely they still didn't get it.

They were so inculcated with the Messianic thinking of the Pharisees and the teachers of the Law that they couldn't receive the truth when it was slapping them in the face. They were taught from small lads that the Christ would restore to Israel the kingdom of David. They would recapture the glory of past eras once again. This cultural expectation led Judas to betray Jesus to the Pharisees. It led the Pharisees to crucify Christ. Even after Christ died and rose from the grave they didn't get it. After 40 days of teaching on the kingdom of God from the risen Christ the disciples asked if this was the time that He would be restoring the kingdom to Israel.

It is amazing how they could have the truth standing before them and so blatantly miss it. It does explain how Christians could embrace Christ and endorse slavery at the same time. How much does this affect our perception of the truth today? Lord, open our eyes to our cultural expectations.

## PART FOUR

**Mark 10:51 "What do you want me to do for you?" Jesus asked him. The blind man said, "Rabbi, I want to see."**

As Jesus left Jericho Bartimaeus, a blind man who was begging by the side of the road, started to call out to Him. The people tried to quiet him but he persisted until he had Jesus' attention. This incident expands on aspects of faith that we can learn from.

The first thing was his persistence. When he knew Jesus was near, he shouted until he was brought into His presence. He didn't give up despite what the crowds were telling him. The same crowd that told him to shut up then encouraged him. One moment they are rebuking him the next patronizing him. Faith needs to push through the fickleness of those around us. Even though people are in the presence of God too they may still try to dissuade us from being so radical. Ignore the crowds and press into Jesus.

When he was called to Jesus, he threw off his cloak. The cloak can represent in that day all that you have, your security, your warmth, and your identity. Hebrews 12:1 says, "let us throw off everything that hinders and the sin that so easily entangles". What are we holding onto that hinders us from receiving from God? Is there sin in our life that we need to repent of? Like the blind man we need to fling those things off in the presence of God.

Getting into Jesus presence wasn't enough to get his miracle. Jesus asked him what he wanted. We sometimes presume that God knows everything we desire so why ask. It seems patently obvious what the man needed but Jesus still asked him. Speaking out what is already birthed in our heart is part of the creative process of releasing faith. He said I want to see.

Jesus said your faith has healed you and immediately he could see. There was no elaborate ceremony or prayer, only the simple words go, your faith has healed you. Faith is the currency of heaven. It provokes a response from God. In everything that happens in the kingdom of God faith has to be involved. Whether it is your faith, the faith of friends or the faith of the crowds, faith must be present for the power of God to be released.

# MARK CHAPTER ELEVEN

# PART ONE

Mark 11:9 – 10   "Those who went ahead and those who followed shouted, "Hosanna!" "Blessed is he who comes in the name of the Lord!" "Blessed is the coming kingdom of our father David!" "Hosanna in the highest!"

The first 11 verses describe Jesus' triumphal entry to Jerusalem with the people cutting palm branches and laying them and their cloaks on the road before him. It was a triumphal entry for the King of Kings and the Lord of Lords but so different from the pomp and ceremony of gentile leaders. The Roman armies would march in with trumpets blaring, full regalia on view, prisoners in tow and the leader riding in a chariot pulled by warhorses.

So, so many things that reflect the kingdom of God are hidden in this story. The supernatural aspect of the kingdom is unveiled through His word of knowledge. He told them where to find the donkey and what to say if people objected. It was exactly as He said. How could He have known other than through the Holy Spirit?

His steed was an unridden donkey, a humble farm animal. It had never been ridden before it carried the King of Kings into Jerusalem. How the Lord uses the lowly and the humble to display His Son to the world. The donkey was tethered and needed to be free. People asked what was happening and the disciples told them the Lord had use for it. Isn't that like us, we are tethered until the Lord sends someone to share the good news to free us. The book of James says He resists the proud but gives grace to the humble.

His army was the common people, who recognized the coming King. They weren't the aristocrats or the leaders but those who were pure of heart. The beatitudes say that blessed are the pure in heart for they will see God. These people were using hosanna as praise, which means saves. They knew that only God could save them. This army would carry His banner forward to conquer the world without raising a weapon. No force could overcome the grace and love of God.

His victory song was the praises of the people. Psalm 22:3 "But You are holy, Enthroned in the praises of Israel". The Lord dwells in the midst of our praises. We bring Him honor and glory when we praise Him. Today as then His victory is declared through our praises. No matter what we see, if we lift up His name in praise, we will see our deliverance for our King cannot resist being in the center of our praise.

Lastly, where did the people come from? There were throngs of them, laying their cloaks or palm leaves before Him. Jesus says in John when I be lifted up I will draw all men to me. How other than through praise can we lift Him up? If we honor Him, He will draw people to Him. Do we need a program to bring them in or do we need heart felt praise?

# PART TWO

**Mark 11:15 - 18 "On reaching Jerusalem, Jesus entered the temple area and began driving out those who were buying and selling there. He overturned the tables of the moneychangers and the benches of those selling doves, and would not allow anyone to carry merchandise through the temple courts. And as he taught them, he said, "Is it not written: '"My house will be called a house of prayer for all nations'? But you have made it 'a den of robbers.'" The chief priests and the teachers of the law heard this and began looking for a way to kill him, for they feared him, because the whole crowd was amazed at his teaching."**

Once again Jesus manages to upset the establishment with his actions. The kingdom of God has a way of doing that. Religion and the kingdom of darkness turn God's house into a place of merchandise. They sell religion and give the impression this is favorable to God. You can pay for indulgences as your way into heaven. Churches sell icons in all kinds of forms to the seekers of God. From statutes to CDs, prayer beads to the latest books are marketed in places of worship. These resources are meant to be aids to growing in God but can take a place of prominence over prayer. As well meaning as our original intent was in providing these supplements to help us they can become a source of income that distracts from the true purpose of the house of God.

God's house was to be a place for all people from all nations to meet with Him. It is still His desire. We meet with Him in prayer. Sometimes in His house we spend more time meeting with each other. It appears that the service is more about pleasing the people than the Lord. We are concerned for how long the worship is, the quality of the message, the need to be inoffensive and to act with proper decorum. We hush God up when He appears through His Holy Spirit. God can be riotous with His kids one meeting and deeply peaceful the next. But how would we know due to our concern to please man? A friend told me that she had been looking and looking for a church where she fit but the Lord told her to look for a church where they allowed Him to fit. Do we do that? Do we merchandise rather than pray?

There is a need for resources that help us in our walk with the Lord. We just need to take special care on how we do it. Does it distract a seeker or does it actually help? Do they think we are about prayer or are they more conscious of our merchandising? Does our merchandising create cultural hindrances to all nations entering the house of God to meet with Him in prayer? Is our church a sanctuary or a tourist site? Ouch!

# PART THREE

**Mark 11:20 "In the morning, as they went along, they saw the fig tree withered from the roots."**

On the way into Jerusalem Jesus was hungry. Going to a fig tree He found there was no fruit as it was not the season for them. Mark 11:14 – "Then he said to the tree, "May no one ever eat fruit from you again." And his disciples heard him say it". The next day it was withered from the roots. Was this a random act or was there something more to it?

The common fig bears a fruit case with the flower within it. To pollinate it there is a fig wasp that goes inside it with the intent of laying its eggs there. The fruit then develops with threads of the flower attached to a seed within. The tree produces 2 and sometimes 3 crops a year. So it was possible for Jesus to see what looked like fruit on the tree from a distance. It was also possible for there to be matured fruit upon the tree.

When He got to it, there was only the shell, no mature fruit to eat. He then spoke to it. This was the week of Passover, which happens on the 15$^{th}$ of the month of Nisan. This month was the first month of the Hebrew calendar and started when the barley harvest was ripe. The fig tree's best fruit was considered the first fruit or spring fruit. Although the barley was ripe, the figs obviously weren't.

So symbolically what did this action speak of? Israel is spoken of as a fig tree. Was He saying that the nation looked fruitful but in reality it wasn't? Was it a reference to the powerlessness of the Sadducees who ruled over the temple? Constantly Jesus' teaching amazed the people as it had authority unlike their teachers of the law. Although the Sadducees and Pharisees were supposed to be the mature, ripe ones who taught others was He saying there was no life in them?

The main thing is the tree withered from the roots. Trees tend to wither from the branches down.

Exceptionally this tree withered from its roots first. The roots determine the quality of fruit. "Do people pick grapes from thorn bushes, or figs from thistles?" (Matthew 7:16)

He spoke to the tree and it died. The kingdom of God exhibits power when words laced with faith are spoken. He went on to tell the disciples that if they had faith in God and did not doubt they could tell a mountain to move and it would. The earth and heavens were formed by the spoken word of God. Jesus spoke and life returned, limbs were healed, eyes could see again, the deaf hear, food multiplied, and fig trees died. Faith in God causes the impossible to become possible. Doubt is the questioning the enemy brings to cause us to stumble in activating our faith. The "what ifs" make us hesitate. It's time to doubt your doubts. The kingdom comes through speaking the word saturated with faith in God.

# PART FOUR

**Mark 11:24 - 25 "Therefore I tell you, whatever you ask for in prayer, believe that you have received it, and it will be yours. And when you stand praying, if you hold anything against**

**anyone, forgive him, so that your Father in heaven may forgive you your sins."**

Jesus says we are to believe that we have received what we prayed for and it will be ours. Conversely we must be able to pray without believing and receive absolutely nothing! Have you ever prayed for something trying to convince yourself that you believe by faith you have it? Deep inside you know you just don't quite believe it. No amount of mental gymnastics can truly convince you that you have it. All of your confessions of having received it by faith sounds phony to your ears and does little to convince your heart that it's true.

We need our prayers to be faith based. Faith births what we pray for. Without faith in our prayers we are simply pleading. All your emotions are not the substance of faith. God responds to faith. Faith has two elements according to Hebrews 11. Faith believes: one, that God is, and two, that He is a rewarder of those who diligently seek Him. Many people believe in God but they don't necessarily believe that they have to diligently seek Him. Faith then gives us a surety of what we are hoping for and a confidence to receive what we don't yet see.

Everything has two creations: one in the thoughts and the other into the natural realm. We are all created because God thought of us first, then we were born. No one who is born is a mistake or an accident. What we pray for needs to be birthed in our spirits first before it becomes a reality here on earth. We need to spend time grappling with God before we have the faith to receive. Jacob wrestled with the angel of the Lord all night long before he received the blessing he so desperately sought. Faith is a gift from God. Sometimes we need to get a hold of Him and not let go until we receive faith for our prayers to be effective.

Faithless prayers go unheeded. Faith filled prayers gives us confidence that we have what we have prayed for. But not forgiving blocks our prayers too! Jesus said if we forgive those we have an issue with, our heavenly Father would forgive our sins. Our heart condition can hinder our prayers. If we have ought against someone, it causes separation. Jesus came to bring reconciliation between God and man, and between each other. Galatians 5:6 states: "For in Christ Jesus neither circumcision nor uncircumcision has any value. *The only thing that counts is faith expressing itself through love."* If faith operates out of the love of God, how can it operate in us if we haven't the love of God in our heart for others? Remember the kingdom of God is activated on earth through faith.

# PART FIVE

**Mark 11:28 "By what authority are you doing these things?" they asked. "And who gave you authority to do this?"**

When the kingdom of God comes in power, people get irritated, particularly the existing religious leaders. The amazing thing about their question is the fact that they recognized His authority. They were upset about it but they still recognized it.

The word, authority, in the Greek is exousia. It means: the power of rule or government (the power of him whose will and commands must be submitted to by others and obeyed). One can have power but not necessarily authority. Authority is bestowed upon you as a responsibility by a higher authority. The police in the UK have authority. Although they are generally not armed, people respond correctly and immediately to the authority bestowed upon them by the Queen and government. Teachers are given authority in schools but not all of them know how to walk in it. One must learn how to use authority, as did the apostles when Jesus sent them out in teams of two.

As believers in Christ you have authority. For it to be effective you have to believe you have it and that you can exercise it. Once you do exert your authority be aware that someone will challenge your right to use it. They will be threatening but don't yield to them or you have lost it. The intent of the questioning is to usurp your authority. You have to be careful not to submit to this attack. You could unintentionally submit yourself to their authority and lose your position of authority in the situation. Spirits are great at trying this bluff. Jealous religious people may certainly try. Things like, oh, we don't pray that way here or we don't believe in public ministry or casting out spirits, can rob your kingdom authority bestowed upon you when you received Christ.

Jesus responded to their questions with a question of His own. They couldn't answer, so neither did He! We need to realize we don't have to answer their questions. If they have to ask, they don't need to know.

# MARK CHAPTER TWELVE

# PART ONE

**Mark 12:10,11:** "The stone the builders rejected has become the capstone; the Lord has done this…"

Jesus told the Pharisees a parable of a vineyard and the landlord's tenants. He said that the owner sent his servants to collect some of the fruit at harvest. They beat or killed the servants. Finally he sent his son who they also killed. The Pharisees knew He was talking about them so what did they want to do? Arrest Him, beat Him, and kill Him!

This parable speaks of the goodness of the owner. Who in their right mind would tolerate tenants who killed or beat one of their servants? But he send servant after servant to them as his emissaries. Our Father has sent his servants, the prophets, to His people over and over again to remind them of whose kingdom it is they serve in, to turn them back to their God. But the people of God stoned them and killed them. He is so full of grace and mercy. No one can accuse Him of being a harsh judge.

The parable also speaks of the fact that the people of God do not own the vineyard. They are servants not owners. The kingdom of God is not ours, yet we often treat the church as if it is. We may piously say that we are only under-shepherds to The Great Shepherd yet by our actions demonstrate ownership. Leaders demand allegiance to their cause and their church and their vision when they are only tenant caretakers of the vineyard.

The parable also points to how atrociously the people of God treat the servants of God. They do not respect the Father who sent them and are very dismissive of those they think are trying to share in the harvest. As we do this to the least of God's people we do it to Him.

# PART TWO

**Mark 12:13-17** **"Later they sent some of the Pharisees and Herodians to Jesus to catch him in his words. They came to him and said, "Teacher, we know you are a man of integrity. You aren't swayed by men, because you pay no attention to who they are; but you teach the way of God in accordance with the truth. Is it right to pay taxes to Caesar or not? Should we pay or shouldn't we?" But Jesus knew their hypocrisy. "Why are you trying to trap me?" he asked. "Bring me a denarius and let me look at it." They brought the coin, and he asked them, "Whose portrait is this? And whose inscription?" "Caesar's," they replied. Then Jesus said to them, "Give to Caesar what is Caesar's and to God what is God's." And they were amazed at him."**

When the religious system (the Pharisees) and the world governmental system (the Herodians) team up together you are in trouble. Neither one appreciates the kingdom of God. They both see it as a threat to their power and position. Under the gentile system position requires people to be subservient and dependent. The government of God calls for people to express their God given authority and dominion over their sphere of the earth. They are to reflect the love of God to all creation. His love is ultimately expressed in free will. To allow that freedom and liberty to be expressed also means that position, status and power are threatened in the eyes of those who hold them.

They came with flattery. Although it was the truth, it was insincere. They were only interested in trapping Jesus so that they could get rid of Him. As His followers we have to be constantly on the alert for this type of entrapment. Proverbs says life and death are in the power of the tongue. If this is so, we need to be careful with our words. Sometimes we need words of wisdom provided by the Holy Spirit or at least the good sense to keep our mouths shut.

Their trap involved the most provocative issue within the world system: taxes. No one likes paying taxes. Everyone is looking for a way to lessen that burden. It was the perfect setup. If your kingdom is opposing Caesar's, then surely we shouldn't have to pay taxes. Jesus was divinely inspired to give the answer He did. Whose inscription is upon the currency? Then give to Caesar what is due to Caesar and give to God what is due to God. The kingdom of God is winning through love and obedience, not rebellion. The apostle Paul said to pray for those who are in power over us. We are to seek to live at peace so that the spread of the gospel is not hindered. Although we are not of the world, we are still in the world. We are leaven that is infecting the whole.

# PART THREE

**Mark 12:24 "Jesus replied, "Are you not in error because you do not know the Scriptures or the power of God?"**

The Sadducees also tried to trap Jesus with a question about the resurrection. They didn't believe in it so they thought they would catch Jesus out. This struck at the very heart of Jesus' purpose. He needed to fulfill the requirements of the law as the last Adam, to take our sin and separation upon His shoulders and pay the price for us: the innocent for the guilty. He spent a great deal of time teaching His disciples about His impending death and resurrection. This act would eradicate Satan's usurpation of authority upon the earth. Satan's system ruling through the fear of death would be defeated through His resurrection. Colossians tells us in verse15 of chapter 2 that Christ having disarmed the powers and authorities made a public spectacle of them, triumphing over them by the cross.

Their intention with the question was to discredit Him publicly. If He disputed with them, they could accuse Him of being with the Pharisees. If He agreed with them, they could entrench their power base over that of the Pharisees. The goal was to undermine His popularity and influence with the people. They wanted to side line Him through political infighting.

His response neither endorsed the Sadducees or the Pharisees. He rebuked them for neither knowing the scriptures nor the power of God. It is interesting that one can know the scriptures and yet not encounter the power of God. The power of God is activated by faith being applied to the scriptures. He said there wouldn't be marriage after the resurrection. The believers will be the Bride of Christ. We won't need a spouse, as He will be our constant lover and companion. In the resurrection we will have unbroken communion with the Father, Son and Holy Spirit.

Mark 12: 26b, 27 says: 'I am the God of Abraham, the

God of Isaac, and the God of Jacob." He is not the God of the dead, but of the living. The religious system lives on past experiences of God. It idolizes those their forefathers killed. It says if we had been there we wouldn't have done that. Yet it rejects a living, dynamic interchange with God now. As they didn't know the scriptures or the power of God they couldn't recognize God with them. If He is alive, we are required to have an active relationship with Him. Many prefer to talk about Him rather than relate to Him for fear He could ask you to lay everything down for Him and His kingdom. In fact the invasion of the kingdom of God does require that but the rewards are so much more than one could ever imagine.

# PART FOUR

**Mark 12:29 – 31 'Hear, O Israel, the Lord our God, the Lord is one. Love the Lord your God with all your heart and with all your soul and with all your mind and with all your strength.' The second is this: 'Love your neighbor as yourself.' There is no commandment greater than these."**

When asked what the greatest commandment was, Jesus responded with love God and love your neighbor as yourself. He didn't refer to the 10 commandments or any other Law of Moses. He spoke of the heart of the matter. If these two commandments are obeyed all the others fall into line. The life of God is one of love not law. Paul said in Galatians 5:14, "The entire law is summed up in a single command: "Love your neighbor as yourself."


Throughout His word the Lord speaks of our proper response to other people. The nation of Israel was to accept the foreigners who chose to live amongst them. They were not to mistreat them but show them mercy and justice as they would a Jew. In the gospels Jesus said as you do to children, or Samaritans, or those in jail you do it unto Him. Our response to others is an indicator of how deeply the love of God abides in our heart.


Paul prays in Ephesians 3:16-19: "I pray that out of his glorious riches he may strengthen you with power through his Spirit in your inner being, so that Christ may dwell in your hearts through faith. And I pray that you, being rooted and established in love, may have power, together with all the saints, to grasp how wide and long and high and deep is the love of Christ, and to know this love that surpasses knowledge--that you may be filled to the measure of all the fullness of

God." The depth of our understanding the love of God is revealed in how we love our neighbors. The love of God does not increase or vary in intensity towards us. The love of God is constant. When we receive Christ, we receive the love of God into our hearts. We have it all but have a limited understanding of how deep and high and wide and long it is towards us. As we walk in the Spirit and in truth we grow in revelation of how much God loves us. We grasp His heart for us. As that happens we respond out of our hearts to others. The word tells us that out of the heart the mouth speaks. It also tells us that the world will know that God sent His son because we love one another.

The entire law is summed up in a single command: "Love your neighbor as yourself." No matter what we say about how we love God, if we don't demonstrate that to other human beings we have yet to grasp the love of God.

# MARK CHAPTER THIRTEEN

# PART ONE

**Mark 13:4 "Tell us, when will these things happen? And what will be the sign that they are all about to be fulfilled?"**

As Jesus was telling His disciples about the future of the temple Peter, James and John asked Him the question. Jesus tells them about the near future and then goes through to His return. Many Christians seem to have an obsession with knowing when the end of time will be. Some organizations hold repeated seminars on the topic as a means to attract people to their community.

Why do we need to know? Could it be we want to be in control of our future? Could it be our security lies in that knowledge rather than a trusting relationship with our Lord? At the end of chapter 12 of Mark when the teacher asked Jesus about the greatest commandments Jesus commended the man as being very close to receiving the kingdom of God because he understood that all the law is summed up in loving your neighbor as yourself. In Matthew 7: 12 Jesus said: "So in everything, do to others what you would have them do to you, for this sums up the Law and the Prophets."

In the early 1980s there was so much teaching about the end times and the coming Rapture and Tribulation. People were told by Christian teachers that their whole organization was living as in the last 5 years of time before Christ's return. There was a book published about the 88 reasons why Christ would return in 88. This whole obsession with the Tribulation created fear, a relatively impotent church and a resultant cocooning within a great number of churches. There was no hope, few would be saved, and we just needed to hang on to the end. The rapture will lift us out of all this evil and then, the Lord can pour out His wrath upon all those unredeemed people.

Where was the greatest commandment to love your neighbor during all this? If this was truly about to happen, why didn't we give every minute of every day sharing our love and faith with others? What happened to the revelation that Jesus was the Christ, the Son of the Living God and upon this revelation He would build His church and the gates of Hades could not overcome it? This end time obsession negated the effectiveness of this command of God for many believers.

As we look at this chapter we will look at it in light of the kingdom of God and faith. Jesus spent His entire ministry including the 40 days after His resurrection teaching on the kingdom of God and its mandate to set the captives free. He was not afraid of the kingdom of Hades, but laid down the battle cry that the gates of Hades would not overcome the church. We are to tear down those gates and set the people free. He shared with us in answer to His disciples' questions what the signs would be to keep us focused on His coming kingdom. Let us look at these signs with faith for the victorious kingdom of God.

# PART TWO

**Mark 13:10-11 "And the gospel must first be preached to all nations. Whenever you are arrested and brought to trial, do not worry beforehand about what to say. Just say whatever is given you at the time, for it is not you speaking, but the Holy Spirit."**

In response to His disciples' questions Jesus said the temple would be destroyed without a stone remaining upon another. He then warned them to be aware of false Christs that would arise to deceive. He said there would be wars, rumors of war, and nations against nations, earthquakes and famines. Believers would be handed over to councils, flogged in religious centers, betrayed by family and all men would hate us. He said when we hear of these things we are not to be alarmed. These things are so clearly evidence of the spiritual warfare to come.

Jesus also said kingdom would be against kingdom. Strong's concordance says the word 'kingdom' ('basileiva') is not to be confused with an actual kingdom but rather the right or authority to rule over a kingdom. Jesus was not talking about a country at war with another country when He used kingdom. He was talking about the conflict between the kingdom of God and the kingdom of darkness. Romans 8:20-21: "For the creation was subjected to frustration, not by its own choice, but by the will of the one who subjected it, in hope that the creation itself will be liberated from its bondage to decay and brought into the glorious freedom of the children of God." All the signs of earthquakes and famines are manifestations of this conflict. Even the earth itself is bound awaiting liberation by the children of God.

When asked by a leader of a denominational church of a certain persuasion what the sign of the baptism of the Holy Spirit was, I responded trouble. He wanted me to answer tongues. But reading the Acts of the Apostles one can see from the time of the outpouring of the Holy Spirit on Pentecost the apostles were changed men who turned the whole world upside down. When they arrived in town, people were polarized. They either hated them or loved them. Often before believing, people violently resist the kingdom of God. The apostle Paul persecuted the church before he received Christ.

In the midst of all these calamities and upheavals Jesus told them they were to preach the gospel to all nations. Gospel means good news. It seems ridiculous that the best news you could ever hear could create such uproar. We must keep all that He said in perspective with His warning of kingdom against kingdom. The enemy of our souls is determined to resist the kingdom of life. In every war there is a turning point where a battle is won that changes the course of the war. Between D Day and VE Day there were more casualties and deaths than in the previous 5 years. D Day was acknowledged as the point when the war swung in favor of the Allies. Our D Day was Easter Sunday. Our VE Day has not yet come but soon. Our purpose is to keep liberating those held captive to the kingdom of Satan.

# PART THREE

**Mark 13:14 "When you see 'the abomination that causes desolation' standing where it does not belong--let the reader understand--then let those who are in Judea flee to the mountains.**

Not to pass this by without a mention, this abomination was considered to be Antiochus Epiphanes. "Antiochus Epiphanes caused an altar to be erected on the altar of burnt-offering, on which sacrifices were offered to Jupiter Olympus. (Compare 1Macc 1:57). This was the abomination of the desolation of Jerusalem. The same language is employed in Daniel 9:27 (Compare Matthew 24:15), where the reference is probably to the image-crowned standards which the Romans set up at the east gate of the temple (A.D. 70), and to which they paid idolatrous honors. "Almost the entire religion of the Roman camp consisted in worshipping the ensign, swearing by the ensign, and in preferring the ensign before all other gods." These ensigns were an "abomination" to the Jews, the "abomination of desolation.""[3]


But the prophecy as spoken by Jesus seems to refer not only to this event but also resonates in this present day. "Given the nature of prophetic utterance, which often includes a more proximate and remote fulfillment, there is no reason why there could not be truth in both of these approaches."[4] Since the destruction of Jerusalem there has not been a temple.

---

[3] Easton's Bible Dictionary:
http://www.biblestudytools.com/Dictionaries/EastonBibleDictionary/ebd.cgi?number=T53

[4] Baker's Evangelical Dictionary of Biblical Theology:
http://www.biblestudytools.com/Dictionaries/BakersEvangelicalDictionary/bed.cgi?number=T4

Even so all the other signs have continued. His word is for all believers to be alert.

Mark 13:22-23: "For false Christs and false prophets will appear and perform signs and miracles to deceive the elect--if that were possible. So be on your guard; I have told you everything ahead of time."

In the midst of all this opposition to the gospel, i.e., the good news of the kingdom of God, there will appear those who will present themselves as the Christ or be false prophets. They will even perform signs and miracles. Why? To deceive the elect! People will resist what is blatantly against their beliefs. To undermine that determination and willingness to sacrifice for the kingdom of God the enemy has and does try to counterfeit with the intention of subtlety leading astray. If he can, he will send his minions to mislead the elect through confusion, idolatry and eventually shipwrecking their faith.

This is war and there are no conventions of war that the enemy respects. We must be on our guard and alert to this possibility. Jesus said in John 4 that the Lord was looking for those who worshipped in Spirit and in truth. We need to rely on and trust the word of God and the Holy Spirit to guide us through the maze of deception that will be thrown at us. He said His sheep know His voice and follow Him. We can rest assured that we know His voice and He will lead us as we seek first the kingdom of God.

# PART FOUR

**Mark 13:34-35 "It's like a man going away: He leaves his house and puts his servants in charge, each with his assigned task, and tells the one at the door to keep watch. "Therefore keep watch because you do not know when the owner of the house will come back--whether in the evening, or at midnight, or when the rooster crows, or at dawn.""**

The kingdom of God is exactly like this. Jesus has left His house with each of His disciples in charge. We have an assignment to fulfill whether we see the Lord of the household or not. Our position is to extend the kingdom of God, His house, to include others. We are not to get lax or lazy about it. We really don't know when we will have to give an account to the owner, our King. We have an assigned task that we are responsible for. No one else can do it but you.

Human nature has an amazing ability to adapt and accept all these things Jesus described in chapter 13 as normal. This creates a problem. We lose the edge, as it all seems quite routine and mundane. Life goes on as it always has so why maintain alert status? It is hard to stay constantly alert when nothing seems to be threatening or changing.

Jesus said when the fig tree has leaves and tender twigs you know that summer is near. He said when we see these signs – earthquakes, famines, wars and rumors of war -we know that His return is nearing. In the last decades since Israel bloomed the increase in these phenomena is amazing. We need to live in the tension between His soon coming return and that life goes on. Only the Father knows when He will return. Paul advocated His soon return and 2000 years have passed. Not one of us knows if we will be here when He returns or whether we will go to Him first.

Either way we need to maintain our passion for the mandate of the kingdom of God. We need to share the love that we have so unconditionally and completely received with others. What a tough task! It is when you consider that people will hate you and react to you until the revelation of God hits them. We can get very tired of extending ourselves under those circumstances. Faith, that ability to see what is not seen, is so crucial to our receiving the kingdom of God.

# MARK CHAPTER FOURTEEN

# PART ONE

Mark 14:3-5 "She broke the jar and poured the perfume on his head. Some of those present were saying indignantly to one another, "Why this waste of perfume? It could have been sold for more than a year's wages and the money given to the poor." And they rebuked her harshly."

At dinner two days before the Passover a woman anointed Jesus with expensive perfume. The perfume or nard was stored in an alabaster box, which she had to break to release it. Some commentaries say it was the seal that she broke, others the whole box as it was like an ointment and she wanted to get all of it out of the box. This act of worship caused indignation amongst the guests. Jesus rebuked them for their disapproval of her.

Her actions were extravagant by the world's standards. The men saw her as wasting this perfume. She had taken the equivalent of a whole year's wages and squandered it all in one act of worship. The Lord saw it as an act of worship and honor bestowed upon Him. He was not upset about the cost or the extravagance of the offering. He received it as preparation for His burial. She understood what the men with Him never seemed to catch until it was done. She poured out her savings in one lavish act of love to the one who unconditionally loved her.

The criticism is cloaked in religious and pious overtones. This money could have been given to the poor. Jesus said the poor you will have with you always and at any time you could do something good for them. But His presence wasn't going to be with them much longer. The two greatest commandments are: love the Lord your God with all your heart, strength, soul and mind and love your neighbor as yourself. We can't do the second without the first. Without embracing His love for us we are incapable of loving others unconditionally. We will always measure our actions towards others according to what they have or haven't done. She loved Him because He loved her first.

This love calls forth extravagant responses that the world sees as excessive and misplaced. This worship is acceptable to the Lord for He is neither stingy nor frugal. He does not measure out His love in small doses but has loved so deeply and abundantly that He didn't withhold His Son for our sake.

Judas left the table to find an eager audience of conspirators, the Pharisees, who quite gladly agreed a sum for the betrayal of Christ to them. Judas missed the kingdom of God completely. He did not understand that it operates on love and such love calls for great sacrifice. His heart was after a worldly kingdom and so betrayed the one who loved him.

Who can truly understand the depth and the width and the height and the length of God's love for us? Such extravagant love evokes in those who believe excessive, joyous responses that the world will never understand.

# PART TWO

**Mark 14:12 "Where do you want us to go and make preparations for you to eat the Passover?"**

Verses 12 through 31 give the account of the last supper. Jesus flowed in the word of knowledge so amazingly. When they asked Him where to have it, He gave them complete instructions for finding the home. When you enter the city you will find a man carrying a jar of water, follow him. These instructions are clearly not prearranged, as there would have been more specific details. When they go, it is exactly as He said.

At the meal He said one of them would betray Him. They all asked is it I, even Judas Iscariot. Later He said they would all abandon Him. Peter absolutely denies this possibility. So Jesus tells him that he will 3 times before the rooster crows twice. There is a big difference in running for your life versus betraying the Christ. Jesus said it was better to have never been born than to betray Him. There was still redemption for those who fled but not for Judas.

During the meal Jesus took the bread and gave thanks for it. This is known as reciting the special blessing for the mitzvah of matzo. The mitzvah represented the 613 commandments of the Torah and the 7 rabbinic commandments. The term can also refer to the fulfillment of a mitzvah.

Mitzvah has also come to express any act of human kindness, such as the burial of the body of an unknown person. During the Seder meal the bread, matzo, represents their freedom from affliction. Jesus offered His body as the means for our freedom from affliction. What greater love is there than this, to fulfill all the law with an act of incredible kindness?

There were also 4 cups of wine at the meal. The third one stood for 'I will redeem". It was also known as the cup of blessing. Jesus said, "This is my blood of the covenant, which is poured out for many." Every person at the meal is to drink from this cup. Jesus said He wouldn't drink of it again until He drinks it anew in the kingdom of God. We who receive His blood sacrifice are blessed.

To bring the kingdom of God Jesus had to fulfill all that the Passover meal stood for. He is our freedom and our blessing.

# PART THREE

**Mark 14:38 "Watch and pray so that you will not fall into temptation. The spirit is willing, but the body is weak."**

After the last supper Jesus and the disciples went to the Garden of Gethsemane to pray. He asked His disciples to watch and pray. Eyes open, alert! What was the temptation they needed to avoid? I think it was not to succumb to slumber. Often when spiritual warfare is the most intense, the body cannot sustain the pace. The body becomes especially fatigued in times of great spiritual intensity. The spirit is willing but the body fails us. When one is engaged in spiritual activity, it is taking its toil on the body physically. We are not detached parts but whole. Each part – spirit, soul and body – affects the other. In times of revival or great spiritual activity as disciples of the Lord we need to be vigilant to rest to sustain the race over the long haul.

The intensity of His situation was overwhelming. To think of the agony He went through knowing that soon He would be turned over to the Sanhedrin to be put to death is heartrending. If there was any time He needed someone praying for Him this was the time.

"My soul is overwhelmed with sorrow to the point of death", He said. He knew what the prophets had described would happen. He was fully human and desired to do anything but this. Some times we make it sound so easy for Him when we preach about His sacrifice, His death. The sorrow almost killed Him! He asked if they could be any other way. His choice was to submit to the Father's will not His own. At that point He could have failed to go through with it. It wasn't forced on Him. He did choose to go along with the Father's will. That same choice Adam failed to make in the Garden. He failed to align with the Lord's will but Christ didn't fail us. He completed as the last Adam what the first Adam didn't do.

# PART FOUR

**Mark 14:44-45 "Now the betrayer had arranged a signal with them: "The one I kiss is the man; arrest him and lead him away under guard." Going at once to Jesus, Judas said, "Rabbi!" and kissed him."**

Judas was one of the twelve, selected by Jesus after a night in prayer. He was never excluded from the inner circle nor ostracized at any time. He was given the responsibility of being the treasurer for the group, a place of trust. Three years he was a constant companion to Christ. Did he think from the beginning that he would betray Christ? I doubt it. His heart turned when he realized that Jesus' kingdom was not going to restore Israel to its former glory under David and Solomon. Jesus rebuked Peter publicly for having his heart set on the things of man. Each of the disciples had a desire for earthly glory and position. No one knows the heart of man except the Lord. Did Jesus know Judas' heart from the beginning? He knew that all men's hearts were evil and that He could trust no one. Even so He loved all of them.

His emotional pain in this betrayal is very real. Hebrews 2:18 states: "Because he himself suffered when he was tempted, he is able to help those who are being tempted." Seated at the right hand of the Father in heaven is a man who suffered in all ways as we have. He understands our pain and our responses. He understands when we want to run away or to lash out. He is not indifferent to our temptations but is always available to help us in our time of need.

The psalmist wrote prophetically of Jesus in Psalm 55:13, 14: "But it is you, a man like myself, my companion, my close friend, with whom I once enjoyed sweet fellowship as we walked with the throng at the house of God." Jesus said His kingdom would set brother against brother, mother against daughter and father against son. As we embrace His kingdom we will experience times when those we thought were our companions, our close friends, will turn against us. There is only one way to deal with that pain. Go to the one who has suffered and is ever making intercession to the Father on our behalf. He understands and empathizes with the pain and rejection. We can be bitter or better. Our decision to go or not to go to Him will make all the difference.

# PART FIVE

**Mark 14:31 "But Peter insisted emphatically, "Even if I have to die with you, I will never disown you." And all the others said the same".**

Through this chapter there are two stories overlaid. One is the story of Judas and his betrayal of Christ;

the other is Peter and his denial of Christ. There are far more verses dedicated to Peter's situation than to what Judas did. It could be that Mark was a relative of Peter's and is considered to have recited Peter's version of events. In that case Peter could have been sharing his remorse with the readers. But if we believe the Holy Spirit inspired the writing of the bible then the emphasis in this Gospel is His work. What is He trying to tell us?

Peter was determined to be loyal to Christ no matter what. He cut off the ear of the high priest's servant in the garden. He was ready to fight even though badly outnumbered. He followed the procession at a distance, even to entering the grounds of the high priest's house. Yet when confronted by a servant girl he buckled in his determination. He denied Christ three times when he was identified as being part of His crew. When the rooster crowed a second time, verse 72 says he broke down and wept.

Is the Holy Spirit trying to show us that out of our good intention and the strength of our determination we will fail? Following the Lord requires an anointing of power from on high. John the Baptist foretold that Jesus would come baptizing in the Holy Spirit and in power. When He rose from the dead He spent

40 days with His disciples teaching them about the kingdom of God. He then told them to wait in Jerusalem for the baptism of the Holy Spirit. Verse 8 of Acts 1 He said, "But you will receive power when the Holy Spirit comes on you; and you will be my witnesses in Jerusalem, and in all Judea and Samaria, and to the ends of the earth."

When that happened Peter was a transformed man. He spoke in front of thousands a message of repentance for the kingdom of God was at hand. Thousands were baptized in response to his message. He was empowered by the Holy Spirit. What he couldn't do in his own strength and courage, he could under the unction of the Holy Spirit. It is requisite for believers to do the works of the kingdom, not just talk about it.

# PART SIX

**Mark 14:62-63 "I am," said Jesus. "And you will see the Son of Man sitting at the right hand of the Mighty One and coming on the clouds of heaven." The high priest tore his clothes. "Why do we need any more witnesses?" he asked."**

At His trial no witnesses could be found that agreed on any point of law. Out of desperation the high priest asked Him if He were the Christ, the Son of the Blessed One. Jesus answered only to this question throughout the trial. He answered, 'I am'. With that the high priest and everyone with him condemned Jesus to death. They called it blasphemy, which Strong's defines as impious and reproachful speech injurious to divine majesty.

His speech only agreed with what His Father had said to Him at His baptism with John. "You are my son in whom I am well pleased". Jesus could not deny the truth but they could not stand to hear it. What kept them so blind to the revelation that He was the Christ? The people got it but the leaders didn't. There in is the rub. They were envious of His popularity with the people. Envy blinds you from seeing what is blatantly obvious to everyone else.

King Saul was fine with David until the women sang that Saul had slain his thousands but David his ten thousands. At that point Saul thought what more could he want but the kingdom. Envy entered into his heart and he was consumed with a desire to kill

David. His own son, Jonathan, the heir to the throne could see that David was God's choice to rule over the kingdom. Jonathan's love for David and willingness to relinquish his position to him infuriated Saul. Saul ended life a broken man under attack and out of touch with God. It was far from a glorious finish to his reign.

Years later the same spirit of envy arose in the religious leaders with the same intent: to kill the son of David, an heir to the throne. Herod saw Jesus as a threat when He was born. He had all the boys two and under put to death to eliminate any possibility of Jesus overthrowing him. Now 30 years later the religious leaders were putting Him to death to preserve their place. In this situation they were only able to do what Christ allowed them to do. He said I lay my life down, no man takes it from Me. In the Garden He said to Peter He could call upon the Lord and He would send a legion of angels to deliver Him. But He knew this was the time and He laid His life down.

# MARK CHAPTER FIFTEEN

# PART ONE

**Mark 15:9 – 11 "Do you want me to release to you the king of the Jews?" asked Pilate, knowing it was out of envy that the chief priests had handed Jesus over to him. But the chief priests stirred up the crowd to have Pilate release Barabbas instead.**

The envy of the religious leaders had already spilled out in their beating of Jesus before they took Him to Pilate. Their envy turned Him over to Pilate who though he saw through it still sought to please the people. Envy empowered the Pharisees to turn the people against Christ and to ask for the release of a murderer in the person of Barabbas. Envy pushed Pilate to have Christ scourged and beaten by the Roman soldiers.

Isaiah 53:11-12: "After the suffering of his soul, he will see the light of life and be satisfied; by his knowledge my righteous servant will justify many, and he will bear their iniquities… For he bore the sin of many, and made intercession for the transgressors." Isaiah prophesied that the Messiah would take our iniquities and sins upon Himself. He bore them for us. He who was without sin took our sins as His own. At this time He became the lamb that made atonement for us. He was not only the blood sacrifice; He was also the scapegoat. On the Day of Atonement the high priest would lay his hands upon the head of the scapegoat and confess the corporate sins of the nation. This goat was led into the wilderness, carrying away the sins laid upon it to be remembered no more.

The practice of 'laying on of hands' has a number of applications. One is to impart what you have to another. When the high priest laid hands on the goat he was imparting to the goat all the sins of the nation. Likewise Jesus as the lamb took all the sins of mankind through their taunting and physical abuse.

First the guards at the high priest's home beat him. They imparted the sins of the Jews upon the lamb. Next Pilate had the army beat and scourge Him thus laying the sins of the Gentiles upon Him. He became the innocent one who takes away the sin of the guilty and finished once and for all the need of sacrifices whose blood can never cleanse us from sin. Hebrews 7:27 "Unlike the other high priests, he does not need to offer sacrifices day after day, first for his own sins, and then for the sins of the people. He sacrificed for their sins once for all when he offered himself."

# PART TWO

**Mark 15:26 – 32 "The written notice of the charge against him read: ~the king of the Jews. They crucified two robbers with him, one on his right and one on his left. Those who passed by hurled insults at him, shaking their heads and saying, "So! You who are going to destroy the temple and build it in three days, come down from the cross and save yourself!" In the same way the chief priests and the teachers of the law mocked him among themselves. "He saved others," they said, "but he can't save himself! Let this Christ, this King of Israel, come down now from the cross, that we may see and believe." Those**

**crucified with him also heaped insults on him."**

The end of chapter 14 and through chapter 15 describe the abuse that Jesus endured before He died. They beat Him, scourged Him, spit on Him, drove thorns into His head and plucked His beard from His face. Isaiah 52:14 states: "Just as there were many who were appalled at him-- his appearance was so disfigured beyond that of any man and his form marred beyond human likeness…" He was physically abused to the point of complete exhaustion. To ensure they could crucify Him they forced Simon of Cyrene to carry His cross the rest of the way to Golgotha. There they nail Him to a rough wooden cross. His treatment was so severe that Pilate was surprised when he heard how soon Jesus had died. For the sake of you and me and the kingdom of God He endured the beatings rather than call His Father to send a legion of angels to rescue Him.

When He hung on the cross He was mocked by those who passed, by the chief priests and teachers of the law, and by the robbers on each side of Him. They called Him the Christ, the King of Israel, and taunted Him with pledges of worship if He came down off the cross. They mocked. To mock is to tease or laugh at in a scornful or contemptuous manner.

Mocking is hostile in intent. They laughed at the Lord. He chose to endure their scorn rather than call upon His Father for deliverance.

They thought that they were eradicating any threat to their kingdom of self. Satan thought he was putting an end to any threat to his kingdom of darkness. They mocked the King of the Jews, celebrating their victory with ridicule. For the kingdom to come, for the keys of death and Hades to be snatched from the evil one, for life and life more abundantly to be available, for the Comforter to come He had to endure.

And He endured!

Praise God He endured!

# MARK CHAPTER SIXTEEN

# PART ONE

**Mark 16:8 "Trembling and bewildered, the women went out and fled from the tomb. They said nothing to anyone, because they were afraid".**

Three women, Mary Magdalene, Mary the mother of James, and Salome, had gone to anoint Jesus' body for burial. The last thing they were expecting was an angel with a message. Trembling seems to be a very natural reaction to angelic visitations. They said nothing to anyone because they were afraid.

They were afraid people would think they were out of their minds. They were afraid of the repercussions of the Romans, as they were assigned to guard the tomb so His disciples would not steal the body away. What would they do when they realized the body was missing? They were afraid of the religious leaders who had Him crucified. If they did that to Jesus, what will they do to us who report Him gone? They could only rationalize within their life context, as they hadn't really believed what He said about His death and resurrection.

Their worldview was totally askew. Your worldview is the framework within which you interpret what your senses are relaying to you. Anointing a dead body was normal as was life and death. But as the disciples struggled every time Jesus talked about His death and resurrection so did these women.

He then appeared to Mary Magdalene but no one believed her. He appeared in another form to disciples along the road to Emmaus. When they told everyone the disciples still didn't believe the truth. Our worldview can cause us to deny a phenomenon that happens right before our very eyes. Our worldview is engrained in us from childhood. It is fully shaped by our culture. If no one had done it before, then it can't be done.

The kingdom of God calls believers to live by faith. Faith calls into existence that which is unseen and hoped for. As God's faith created the heavens and the earth, His faith still creates. When we align with His faith, things we have never seen before can be brought into existence. The bible gives us some dynamic possibilities that the Body of Christ still struggles with. One part of the body will pray for divine healing, another part will deny that it is possible. The bible says with faith we will see the dead raised, yet most of church culture due to a lack of deeds expresses to us that it doesn't happen today.

In verse14 it says: "Later Jesus appeared to the Eleven as they were eating; he rebuked them for their lack of faith and their stubborn refusal to believe those who had seen him after he had risen". He rebuked them. Rebuke means to express sharp disapproval or criticism of someone because of their behavior or actions. Jesus was not pleased with them. Here He was entrusting them with the mission of bringing the kingdom of God to all the earth and they were stubbornly refusing to believe. Only faith receives the kingdom and that faith propagates the kingdom. Amen!

# PART TWO

**Mark 16:20 "Then the disciples went out and preached everywhere, and the Lord worked with them and confirmed his word by the signs that accompanied it."**

Mark in his usual efficiency summed up Jesus' finally words in four verses. Verses 15 - 18 "He said to them, "Go into all the world and preach the good news to all creation. Whoever believes and is baptized will be saved, but whoever does not believe will be condemned. And these signs will accompany those who believe: In my name they will drive out demons; they will speak in new tongues; they will pick up snakes with their hands; and when they drink deadly poison, it will not hurt them at all; they will place their hands on sick people, and they will get well." Although some versions of the bible say later manuscripts added the verses after verse 8 in chapter 16, there is nothing in these words that contradicts anything Jesus said as recorded in the Gospels.

His words were 'go and preach'. When you preach people will be saved. Paul says in Romans that the gospel is the power of God unto salvation. As we preach His word there will be supernatural confirmations of what you are preaching. These signs are to secure your faith in the power of God, not in the words of man. There are so many different messages preached to capture the attention of people or to create confusion so the right message is ignored. The key to the kingdom of God is faith releasing the power of God when the gospel is preached.

There have been many approaches in recent years to evangelism. Although they may catch a person's attention, they still need to hear the gospel. Is the gospel clear? Is His word being confirmed by signs?

If there aren't any signs, maybe we are missing the Lord working with us? We can go everywhere and preach but did we go where the Lord directed us? Paul and his crew tried to go into Asia but the Spirit stopped them over and over again. Then he had a dream of a man in Macedonia beckoning him for help. In the morning he related the dream to his team and they headed for Macedonia. Up until then, he was trying to go and to preach but he didn't have the Lord working with him.

Mark's gospel is one of action. He began by

portraying Jesus as a man of action. He concludes with Jesus, the man of action, saying: 'go'. As He went to the people with the message of the kingdom of God He expects us to go too. Where did God say 'go to' for you? Then do it in faith and watch the Lord confirm your words with signs that point to the truth of what you have said. The kingdom of God comes to those who receive it by faith. Expect it!

# ABOUT THE AUTHOR

Jim is a spiritual entrepreneur. He has asked the question "Why can't we?" throughout his Christian walk. Over and over the Lord has answered, "yes, you can." Jim has pastored churches, planted churches, started leadership colleges, co-pioneered a church movement, and developed marriage and parenting seminars with his lovely wife, Bonnie. Together they wrote 24 Secrets to Great Parenting.

Jim is an author and international speaker. He has a Father's heart and has four wonderful children of his own and a great many spiritual children.

His greatest passion is to teach others how to "do the stuff" of the Kingdom of God. 2 Timothy 2:2, "And the things you have heard me say in the presence of many witnesses entrust to reliable men who will also be qualified to teach others", has been his life's inspiration.

# OTHER BOOKS AND RESOURCES BY JIM INKSTER

## The Heart of the Matter
(Paperback)

The Heart of the Matter is an interesting journey into the heart of God and our response to His amazing unconditional giving. It reveals excellent revelation and insight into the heart of our heavenly Father.

**Available through Amazon, CreateSpace e-store and Kindle**

## Eyes of Wonder
(paperback)

Eyes of Wonder is a delightful collection of life experiences with the children and grandchildren that have taught Jim everything he needed to know to be an adult.

Similar to the Chicken Soup for the Soul series this gives you simple downhome wisdom. Always good for a chuckle too!

**Available through Amazon and on Kindle.**

## Faith: The Currency of Heaven
(Paperback)

This is a bible study on faith and it's application today. Each chapter is written to stand on its own so that you can either sequentially work through the study or randomly pick and choose chapters. It is a must read book for those seeking to live a life by faith.

**Available through Amazon, CreateSpace e-store or Kindle**

# BOOKS AND RESOURCES BY JIM AND BONNIE INKSTER

## 24 Secrets To Great Parenting
(Paperback)

Jim and Bonnie share from their vast experience the principles that helped them raise four great children. It is written in a light-hearted, easy reading style perfect for the busy parent with very little spare time on their hands.

**Available through Amazon, CreateSpace e-store and on Kindle**

## 8 Questions Every Parent Wants Answered (DVD)

Jim and Bonnie surveyed hundreds of parents to find what issues are their greatest concern regarding their children. Eight questions were consistent from parents throughout the world.

These questions have been addressed in a powerful and entertaining format. Each session takes less than 10 minutes with great ideas for successful application within your family.

**Soon to be available through Amazon**

## 24 Secrets to Great Parenting
(Audiobook)

Jim and Bonnie felt that this great book had to be available to everyone including those who don't like to read. The research shows men prefer to listen, women prefer to read.

Jim was professionally studio recorded reading this charming and helpful book. Great for in the car or on your personal player when exercising or simply chilling!

**Soon to be available through Amazon**

## The Christmas Story
(Paperback)

The Christmas Story is a fresh perspective on Christ's birth through the Gospel writings of Matthew and Luke. Jim looks at the story from Matthew's perspective, which seems reflective of Joseph's side of the story. Bonnie writes about the birth from Luke and what is very strongly focused on Mary's perspective of the event.

The Christmas Story is a great devotional with one section for each of the 12 days before Christmas or a thought provoking bible study. Highly recommended for a fresh look at a familiar story!

**Available through Amazon, CreateSpace e-store or Kindle**

# BOOKS AND RESOURCES BY BONNIE INKSTER

## Under His Wings
(Paperback)

This is a wonderful devotional written on Psalm 91. Each verse is explored through cross-referencing and illustrations from God's word. Ideal for personal study one chapter at a time or read all at once. The word of God is active, alive and very, very effectual in bringing us encouragement to live by in this present day. Don't miss it!

**Available through Amazon, CreateSpace e-store or Kindle**

# Great Blogs

http://www.jimandbonnie.co.uk
Jim and Bonnie write a weekly blog giving thoughtful and sometimes witty insights into relationships, marriage and parenting.

http://www.gatewaysministries.com

http://www.jimandbonnieinkster.com

Jim and Bonnie can be contacted through these websites.

Don't miss any of them!!

www.ingramcontent.com/pod-product-compliance
Lightning Source LLC
LaVergne TN
LVHW051600070426
835507LV00021B/2676